The Lord bless you and keep you;
The Lord make His face shine upon you,
And be gracious to you;
The Lord lift up His countenance upon you,
And give you peace.

'So they shall put My *name* on the children of Israel, and I will bless them.'

Numbers 6:24–27 NKJV

Name Covenant: Invitation to Friendship
Strategies for the Threshold #3

© Anne Hamilton 2018

Published by Armour Books
P. O. Box 492, Corinda QLD 4075

Cover Image: © RyanJLane/istockphoto; © Can Stock Photos/
innovatedcaptures
Section Divider Image: © Can Stock Photo/100ker
Interior Design and Typeset by Book Whispers

ISBN: 978-1-925380-132

 A catalogue record for this
book is available from the
National Library of Australia

Strategies for the Threshold #3

Name Covenant:
Invitation to Friendship

Anne Hamilton

Other Books By Anne Hamilton

In this series

Dealing with Python: Spirit of Constriction
Dealing with Ziz: Spirit of Forgetting

Devotional Theology

God's Poetry: The Identity & Destiny Encoded in Your Name
God's Panoply: The Armour of God & the Kiss of Heaven
God's Pageantry: The Threshold Guardians & the Covenant Defender
God's Pottery: The Sea of Names & the Pierced Inheritance
God's Priority: World-Mending & Generational Testing
More Precious than Pearls:
The Mother's Blessing & God's Favour Towards Women
(with *Natalie Tensen*)

Mathematics and Theology in Medieval Poetry

Gawain and the Four Daughters of God:
the testimony of mathematics in Cotton Nero A.x

Award-winning Children's Books

Many–Coloured Realm
Daystar: The Days are Numbered Book 1
Merlin's Wood: The Battle of the Trees 1

Thank you

Sarah

Martina (Mary)

Janine

Janice

Janne

Josie

Anna

Anne Marie

Michael

Donna

Quang

Willem

Arie

and my very special mum, Dell

Contents

1	**The Welcome of Strangers**	1
2	**Heart of My Own Heart**	19
3	**A Wrestle with Angels**	45
4	**Shuttering Heaven**	81
5	**Naming His Names**	117
Appendix 1	**Summary**	139
Appendix 2	**Name Covenants in Scripture**	143
Appendix 3	**Remembering Names**	146
Appendix 4	**Naming For Unresolved Family Issues**	148
Appendix 5	**Oath Brothers**	151
Appendix 6	**Model Prayers**	156
Appendix 7	**Further Reading**	160
Endnotes		163

About this series

This book is the third in a series outlining strategies for passing over into your calling. Without a basic understanding of name and threshold covenants, you'll find you get walloped every time you approach the spiritual doorway into the destiny God has prepared for you.

I don't pretend to know everything there is to know about name and threshold covenants. So test what I say. Go to God and ask Him. When it comes to names, their very uniqueness means there are no hard-and-fast rules. That means there is definitely no certainty the meaning listed in any modern book about names is God's view of the matter. I speak through experience. Until recently I had no doubt whatsoever the definition of 'Mary' and its variants was as solid and unassailable as could be. There might have been other names I've had suspicions about over the years but it never ever crossed my mind there could be any as-yet-undiscovered meaning for Mary that wasn't part of our common cultural knowledge bank. Let alone that this meaning was actually God's perspective on it. All I had by way of doubt was sufficient understanding of name covenants to realise that somewhere in the following words was God's meaning for the name: *'Truly I tell you, wherever this gospel is preached throughout the world, what she has done will also be told, in memory of her.'* It took eighteen months to find the meaning—in retrospect, the oh-so-obvious meaning—along with its surprising etymological path.

So, if you get half-way through this book and think that you need to ask me what the true meaning of your name is, don't. Just don't. I'm happy to receive questions at any time—but there is only one authority on the meaning of your name and that's God. Ask Him. And keep asking Him.

Because this book is part of a series, it focuses on just one aspect of thresholds. If you're looking for a general overview of threshold covenants, please allow me to suggest both *God's Pageantry* and *God's Pottery* which are both part of an allied series. People often ask me which of my books they should read first. My answer is: 'Start anywhere, except *God's Pottery*. Don't read it until after you've read *God's Pageantry*.' If you are interested in overcoming the threshold guardians who block your way into your calling, consider the books on the spirits of constriction and forgetting: *Dealing with Python* and *Dealing with Ziz*.

And should you be looking for more on this same topic of name covenants, though in a more generalised fashion, allow me to recommend *God's Poetry*. Be warned, however: it's not as linear in construction as this book—it deliberately tries to jolt you out of the scientific rationalist thinking you aren't aware you have.

Be blessed as you read. May your name be brought into union with His—and His favour rest on you evermore.

Introduction

More than a century ago, Henry Clay Trumbull wrote three hugely popular works on the blood covenant, the salt covenant and the threshold covenant. He also mentioned his plans to follow them up with a similar volume on name covenants. But, as far as I can tell, the projected publication never happened.

Trumbull was a world-famous editor and author as well as a pioneer of the Sunday School movement. His books on covenant quite naturally reflect their own era, so they have a studied, anthropological approach—that is, they describe the practice of covenant as it still existed in different cultures around the world at that time. In the light of those contemporary customs, he went on to examine numerous Scriptural passages. The insights offered by this method were invaluable.

So, following in his footsteps, the first part of this book looks at the practice of name covenanting in the last few centuries—and what we can learn about Scripture through the remaining vestiges of the practice.

Just how significant are name covenants? How many are actually recorded in Scripture?

That's not as easy to answer as it might seem. There are,

of course, some that are so blatant they are unmissable—Abram becomes Abraham, Jacob becomes Israel, Simon becomes Peter, and Saul becomes Paul. These spell out in explicit detail the circumstances of when and where the covenant occurred.

But there are other more subtle ones, lurking in the background, waiting for us to decipher the clues that must have been obvious in past ages but tend to zoom right over us today. These include Sarah, Joseph, Phinehas, Joshua, Gideon, Solomon and Mary Magdalene. There are at least a dozen examples in Scripture and perhaps as many as two dozen.

You might want to skip straight to the section that addresses the Scriptural examples. Or you might want to join me in following the approach of Henry Trumbull to see what a name covenant has looked like in the last few centuries.

Anne Hamilton

Brisbane, Australia 2018

PS—As usual, this entire book is designed using 'numerical literary style', a word-number fusion similar to that found throughout medieval manuscripts and the Christian Scriptures. This means that each section is crafted to be a specific word length, usually a multiple of 111, *the number of covenant*, or in the proportion known as the golden ratio, *the number of creation*. Both 111 and the golden ratio are found in Genesis 1:1 with its embedded name covenant.

1

The Welcome of Strangers

You are to imagine a four-wheeled gig; one horse; in the front seat two Tahiti natives in their Sunday clothes, blue coat, white shirt, kilt (a little longer than the Scotch) of a blue stuff with big white or yellow flowers, legs and feet bare; in the back seat me and my wife who is a friend of yours; under our feet, plenty of lunch and things: among us a great deal of fun in broken Tahitian, one of the natives, a sub-chief of the village being a great ally of mine. Indeed we have exchanged names; so that he is now Rui, the nearest they can come to Louis, for they have no L and no S in their language. Rui is six feet three in his stockings, and a magnificent man. We all have straw hats, for the sun is strong. We drive between the sea, which makes a great noise, and the mountains; the road is cut through a forest mostly of fruit trees, the very creepers which take the place of our ivy, heavy with a great and delicious fruit, bigger than your head and far nicer, called Barbedine. Presently we came to a house in a pretty garden, quite by itself, very nicely kept, the doors and windows open, no one about, and no noise but that of the sea. It looked like a house in a fairy-tale, and just beyond we must ford the river, and there we saw the inhabitants. Just in the mouth of the river, where it met the sea waves, they were ducking and bathing and screaming together like a covey of birds: seven or eight little naked brown boys and girls as happy as the day is long; and on the banks of the stream beside them, real toys—toy ships, full rigged and with their sails set, though they were lying in the dust on their beam ends. And then I knew for sure we were all children in a fairy-story, living alone together in that lonely house with the only toys in all the island; and that I myself had driven, in my four-wheeled gig, into the corner of the fairy-story, and the question was, should I get out again? But it was all right; I guess only one of the wheels of the gig had got into the fairy-story; and the next jolt the whole thing vanished, and we drove on in our sea-side forest as before, and I have the honour to be Tomarcher's valued correspondent, TERIITERA, which he was previously known as

Robert Louis Stevenson[1]

The year was 1888. Acclaimed children's writer, Robert Louis Stevenson, author of *Treasure Island* and *The Strange Case of Dr Jekyll and Mr Hyde*, had come to the South Pacific. Writing back home to a friend's small son, Tom Archer, he mentioned a name covenant he'd undertaken with a local chief. Of course he didn't use that

2

terminology with its ancient Biblical echoes. However it's clear from subsequent events that's exactly what it was.

Stevenson had arrived in Tautira, a small corner of the island paradise of Tahiti, desperately sick from a chronic illness. There he was befriended by Princess Moë, a woman of great and stately beauty who spoke impeccable English. She found him lodging and helped nurse him back to health with fish delicacies cooked in coconut milk and lime juice. Stevenson's wife, Fanny, firmly believed Princess Moë saved his life, and she asked this royal grandmother to introduce him to the chieftain Ori a Ori.

Princess Moë conveyed Fanny's request for a name exchange to Ori, who responded with a cordial offer of brotherhood: 'So now, if you please, Louis is no more Louis, having given that name away in the Tahitian form of Rui, but is known as Terii-Tera.'[2]

Ori a Ori was apparently a clan title and Teriitera the chief's personal name. In an earlier generation, the great English explorer James Cook had exchanged names with another Ori a Ori. Accepting name exchanges had in fact been Cook's regular practice wherever he dropped anchor for any length of time. Yet even before he'd voyaged across the Pacific, the benefits of these friendship ceremonies were well-known to European sailors. The advantages of going through a *taio*[3] ritual and exchanging names were obvious: the foreigners were no longer considered strangers but family. According to Stevenson's letters, the newly named Rui informed him: 'You are my brother: all that I have is yours. I know that your food is done, but I can give you plenty of fish and taro.'[4]

All that I have is yours: such was the obligation of *taio* to one another. The sentiment expressed by these words was typical of the deepest kind of friendship known to the ancient world: that of covenant.

Taio friends were to be protected, even at great personal risk. The very day after the name exchange with Stevenson, Rui sailed to Papeete, the main town of Tahiti, 'amidst a raging sea and a storming wind'[5] to collect European food supplies for the visitors.

The concept of *taio* was widespread across the Pacific. Cook had exchanged names with the Tahitian high chief, Tu, as well as the regent, Tutaha. He'd also exchanged names with Ori a Ori, governor of the island Huahine, and with Reo, governor of Raiatea.

In the kingdom of Tonga he'd exchanged names with Ataonga; on Tongatapu itself with the young chief Waheiadoo. Members of his crew also participated in *taio* rites—on his third voyage, for example, Charles Clerke exchanged names with a young Tahitian woman Poorahi. And prior to Cook's voyages, an earlier explorer, Samuel Wallis of the HMS *Dolphin,* had become the *taio* of Purea whom the British considered the queen of Tahiti at the time.

Sometimes, though far from always, such *taio* friendships might involve sexual intimacy—as George Hamilton discovered when his new bond with Matuara, the king of York Island, involved bedding the queen.[6]

One of the advantages of *taio* was the avoidance of conflict, the easing of suspicion and the smoothing of the path into various trading and commercial enterprises.

But conflict could be the direct result of *taio* too. It's very likely James Cook's death in Hawaii was due to his failure to understand the deeper nuances of these relationships. He had exchanged names—and a cloak and feather helmet for a sword and a linen shirt—with Kalaniʻōpuʻu. The chief then called himself 'Kuki' and Cook used the name 'Terreeoboo' which seems about the closest he could come to pronouncing Kalaniʻōpuʻu.

This exchange of clothing items was a typical, but not universal, part of the ceremony. It is highly reminiscent of the exchange of mantles during a covenant ceremony in Hebrew culture—and with much the same meaning: to bring the outsider into the clan or tribe and bestow on them privileges and obligations to be fulfilled as part of their new family.

Now the name exchanges Cook had made with various local aristocrats may have facilitated his path across the societies of the Pacific through three long voyages. However they had also brought him 'into a continuum of kinship, ancestry and creation beings. He exchanged names, titles and power with chiefs who were at the godly end of the continuum, and in being transformed from stranger to kin, he was also brought into relationship with ancestors and other figures of power.'[7] So, when he arrived back in Hawaii just a few days after a lavish leaving-taking ceremony, he violated the customs of the island. His return was made far worse when he kidnapped his sacred friend, Kalaniʻōpuʻu—and thus found himself on the receiving end of savage retaliation.

Name exchanges were by no means restricted to the captains of expeditions. Lieutenant George Tobin felt privileged to accept an offer of *taio* made to him by Queen 'Itia of Tahiti in 1792. Just three years earlier in the same place, Fletcher Christian exchanged names with the chief Tummotoa. This was just a few months after Christian had instigated the infamous 'Mutiny on the *Bounty*' and set the captain, William Bligh, adrift in an open launch.

Captain Bligh himself had previously pressed noses with Pōmare I, the unifier and first overall king of Tahiti. They had also exchanged names: 'Bry' (or 'Parai'—apparently the closest pronunciation the islanders could manage to 'Bligh') in return for 'Tinah', one of the names Pōmare was using at the time.[8] It was understood this exchange meant Bligh shared Pōmare's name, lineage, ancestors and network of enmities and alliances on the island.[9]

Nor were name exchanges restricted to Tahiti. Edward Robarts served aboard a whaler until he jumped ship in 1798 in the Marquesan Islands. He remained there for eight years, exchanging names with a prominent landowner, Kiatonui, and marrying his daughter. His stay overlapped that of William Pascoe Crook, a missionary, who also exchanged names with Kiatonui. Crook's evangelising efforts met with a puzzled response in this remote archipelago: 'How can Mr Crook claim to know God, when he cannot even tell one tree from another?'

In the Marquesas, this kind of friendship is not called *taio* but *e inoa*. Older documents however refer to it as *taeehs* or *teii*. As late as 1903, *e inoa* was still a significant aspect of Marquesan culture. The impressionist painter Paul

Gauguin was living in the islands at the time—having come there from Tahiti two years previously. However his health was deteriorating so fast that even he recognised he had very little time to live. His legs were covered with ulcers; the pain was so agonising even morphine was ineffective. His eyesight had been ravaged by syphilis. The locals nicknamed him 'Koke', *wattle-daub*. This was his *patiki*—an insulting name customarily bestowed on a person during their first tattoo.

Gauguin had employed a highly skilled local carpenter, Tioka, *scooped-out*, to build him a two-storey beach house. It was so well-constructed that it was one of the very few dwellings to survive a devastating cyclone. Koke and Tioka became bond-friends, *e inoa*. As the sight and smell of Gauguin's suppurating skin drove others away, only his *e inoa* remained faithful to the very end.

Greg Dening comments: 'Exchanging names like Wattle-Daub and Scooped-Out might not seem to have much aesthetic appeal. The exchange was a social grace nonetheless. The mutual gift of names embraced the whole person, all the person's rights and obligations, the property. It was never given lightly. It was given between equals but not necessarily between identicals. There was barter in it. Different advantages were exchanged. It was empowering, though. It was political, an alliance in the grassroots of life. It was an alliance steeped as well in all the cultural memories of how things used to be. Exchanging names was a very proper sacrament...'[10]

A very proper sacrament: an outward sign of a spiritual mystery. Dening recognises that, beyond the benefits and advantages to one side or the other, there was a sacred, covenantal nature to this relationship.

Throughout the Pacific, slight variations existed in expectations about bond-friendship. But the concept remained basically the same, even when the name did not. In Tonga it was called *ofa* and in Hawaii, *pili aiki*. In Kiribati it was *kaboara*; and *natam* in Torres Strait. Throughout Polynesia generally it was *tayo* and only in the Society Islands—Tahiti and its neighbours—as well as the Cook Islands around Rarotonga, was it called *taio*.

Taio is of course extraordinarily difficult to translate. It is not by any means culturally unique to the Pacific basin. Over in the Atlantic, in the Caribbean islands of the Antilles, a name exchange was termed *guaitiao*.

Nevertheless the concept has been pushed so far to the margins of the world and has vanished for so long from western society we no longer have any simple way of describing it. Variously rendered as 'bond friend', 'blood brother', 'formal kinship', 'ceremonial comrade', 'friendship contract' or 'sacred friend', *taio* was a solemn exchange involving not only names, identities, rights and obligations. The Hawaiian story *Aka's Voyage for Red Feathers*, mentions two birds Matakia and Vaefati, the *inoa* of the hero, and explains this word as 'name friends'—those with whom one has exchanged names, so that each has claim to the wife and property of the other.[11]

In some places, it was understood that name exchange signified adoption. For example, in Tonga a man who was a chief's *ofa* was considered to have become the son of the chief's mother. In other places, it was considered that roles had been exchanged: one chief who exchanged names with a secular king decided that, thereafter, he had much more latitude when it came to obeying the dictates of the tribal priest.

The example of Paul Gauguin is by no means the last of its type. Name covenants lasted well into the twentieth century. In the 1960s, even as anthropologist Ben Finney was suggesting bond-friendship had apparently died out in Tahiti, he nevertheless reported being invited to observe just such a ceremony. In the process he discovered that *taio*, the word uniformly used across the literature of previous centuries, had fallen into disuse and was completely unknown at the time. Instead *tau'a* or *tau'a-hoa* was used in the rare instances he could uncover of the tradition still existing.

The ceremony he was invited to involved Tehahe, a fisherman, and Tamu, a truck-driver. Apparently, over the course of several congenial beer-drinking sessions, they'd decided they should be buddies for life. Tehahe suggested they become bond-friends; Tamu accepted; the ceremony was arranged and two dozen close friends were invited to the feast. Tamu's family was to provide the pig and wine; Tehahe's kin were to supply fish, vegetables and beer.

A deacon from a local Protestant church began the ceremony by reading from the Bible and 'offering a long prayer about the obligations of mutual aid and life-long faithfulness which Tamu and Tehahe would owe one another as bond-friends.'[12] This was witnessed by their family, kin and friends. Rings were exchanged and then at the close, they exchanged names. Tamu was henceforth to be known as 'Tehahe' and Tehahe thereafter as 'Tamu'. Food was blessed and the new bond-friends sat at the head of the table, sharing in the feast from the same bowl.

Finney, intrigued by what he'd witnessed, made a systematic inquiry about bond-friendship. Although he found only a handful of instances, he was informed that bond-friends could not be related and, despite historical precedents to the contrary, they could not be of the opposite sex. In addition, he was able to establish five common features of the 'making friends' ceremony, *fa'atau'ara'a* or *fa'ahoara'a*:

1. direction by a church official, usually a pastor
2. vows of mutual aid and life-long faithfulness
3. an exchange of rings
4. an exchange of names
5. a feast following

His comment was: 'There are obvious similarities here between the rite of bond-friendship and the modern (Protestant) Tahitian wedding ceremony.'

In fact, the similarities are hardly exclusively Protestant or Tahitian, for that matter. It would be all too easy at this point to overlay a postmodern worldview on this rite and see it as an obvious precursor to today's same-sex marriage ceremony. But just because we don't have any other cultural grid to slot it into does not mean we have to automatically reference it with sexually charged overtones.

'Love' is a catch-all word in English. It is undifferentiated, although it has many nuances and shades. Greek, for instance, is known for distinguishing at least seven words for our one:

- storgē, *maternal* or *familial love*
- érōs, *erotic* or *sexual love*
- ludus, *playful affection*
- philía, *friendship*
- philautia, *self-love*
- pragma, *enduring love*
- agápē, *self-sacrificial love*

And these don't even cover English expressions like: 'I love chocolate' or 'I love weekends' or 'I love the sea.' We slide so fuzzily in our thinking between all sorts of so-called loves—which, in reality, range from mere liking to outright idolising—that we're all too apt to categorise many of them wrongly.

So, although the *fa'atau'ara'a* ceremony looks like a marriage, that's basically because marriage involves covenant. And a covenant is a covenant is a covenant. This is true whether it's name or salt, threshold or blood—or any combination thereof, such as matrimony or that ancient eternal pledge called 'armour-bearing'.

Marriage—generally speaking, of course—still has some aspects of name covenant. When the bride takes a new surname—that of her husband—a partial name exchange occurs. When a child is adopted and a new surname begins to be used, again a partial exchange occurs. Both these instances indicate introduction and incorporation into a wider family.

David Livingstone recorded that the custom of changing names was prevalent among the Manganjas and other tribes of the Zambesi region. One of Livingstone's companions, the headman Sininyane, exchanged names with Moshoshoma, a Zulu. The next morning Sininyane was called but did not answer. He was called again and again, without any response. Finally one of his men explained: 'He is not Sininyane now, he is Moshoshoma.' When called by that name, he answered at once. Livingstone reported: 'The custom of exchanging names with men of other tribes is not uncommon; and the exchangers regard themselves as close comrades, owing special duties to each other ever after. Should one by chance visit his comrade's town, he expects to receive food, lodging, and other friendly offices from him.'[13]

The tribes of the Pacific Coast of North America also practised name exchange. In 1786, Captain Hanna of the *Sea Otter* arrived in the principal Ahousaht village of British Columbia. There he befriended and exchanged names with chief Cleaskinah who subsequently became known as 'Captain Hanna'. As a consequence of this kind of cultural interchange, a sprinkling of foreign names occurred amongst the indigenous chiefs of the north-west.[14] In fact, over a hundred years later in Haida Gwaii—formerly known as the Queen Charlotte Islands—the dynamic native leader Eda'nsa called himself 'Captain Douglas', which he claimed to be a hereditary title descending from the name exchange between Chief Blakow-Coneehaw and Captain William Douglas in 1788.[15]

When Lewis and Clark led their expedition, the first to cross the western part of the United States, into Shoshone territory, they were treated with great honour. Seated on green boughs and antelope skins inside a leather lodge, they shared 'friendly smoke' with Chief Cameahwait and his retinue. During the ceremony, Cameahwait exchanged names with Clark,[16] who thereafter claimed the Shoshones always called him *Ka-me-ah-wah*.[17]

The Japanese also record the custom, though in an unusual fashion. A kami, *an elemental spirit*, wished to exchange names with crown prince Ōjin. During Ōjin's stay in a temporary palace in Tsuruga, the deity Tsunuga ni masu Izasawake appeared in a dream, saying that he wished to exchange his name with that of the prince. The offer was accepted. The spirit then said he would leave offerings on the beach the next morning in return for the prince's name. When the crown prince's retinue visited the beach the following day, they found many porpoises, all with wounded noses. In exchange for this food offering, the crown prince presented the kami with the divine title Miketsu ōkami, *great deity of food offerings*.[18]

In the early days of Australian settlement, many name exchanges took place. The act of exchanging names was called *damoly* or *tamooly* amongst the Eora people. The first governor, Arthur Phillip, was a *damelian*[19] of the famous indigenous warrior, Woollarawarre Bennelong.

Watkin Tench, an officer of the First Fleet, testified: 'He calls the Governor "Beanga", *Father*, and names himself "Doorow", *Son*, and calls the Judge and Commissary "Babunna", *Brother*.' Of his own five names he prefers

Woollarawarre and 'as a mark of affection and respect to the governor, he conferred on him the name of "Wolarawaree"... adopting to himself the name of "governor".[20]

The 'Judge and Commissary' mentioned by Tench was Judge Advocate David Collins, aide to Governor Phillip, who exchanged names with Gnung-a Gnung-a Murremurgan, the husband of Bennelong's sister, Warreeweer. Gnung-a Gnung-a Murremurgan was thereafter called 'Collins' by the English colonists.[21]

Bennelong's second wife, Barangaroo, exchanged names with Daringa, the wife of his friend Colebee. Midshipman Newton Fowell of the First Fleet flagship HMS *Sirius* called him 'Gringerry Kibba Coleby'.[22] His third name, Colebee, came from his exchange with the Gweagal—*fire clan*—warrior Wárungin Wángubile Kólbi.

Colebee's nephew, Nanbarry,[23] exchanged names with Ballooderry, but surrendered that name briefly after Ballooderry's death, adopting instead 'Bo-rahng' (possibly meaning *shadow*).

Another indigenous warrior, Carradah, exchanged names with Henry Ball, who commanded HMS *Supply*. His name however was quickly corrupted to 'Midjer Bool.'[24] Tom Rowley, adjutant of the New South Wales Corps, also exchanged names with a local native man.[25]

According to Keith Vincent Smith, these name exchanges were part of 'a long tradition of reciprocity and kinship,' whereby people forged a relationship similar to the current Australian notion of a 'best mate'. Sharing the same name established a bond of friendship and mutual aid between the namesakes, even those from different clans. He indicates that Woollarawarre Bennelong attempted to find a place for Governor Phillip and his officers in the traditional kinship and skin groups of the Eora people.[26]

William Henry Breton, writing nearly half a century after Tench, reported the custom as being still prevalent with numerous English names amongst people who did not speak a word of the language. 'A soldier of the 57th regiment exchanged names with a leading man in the tribe,' he stated, and the indigenous chief then called himself 'the Duke of York'.[27]

Joseph Gellibrand, the first attorney-general of Tasmania, exchanged names with Barook, the son of the native chief Yagga.[28]

In the mid-nineteenth century, a missionary and industrial schoolmaster named Kennett was invited to Prince of Wales Island in Torres Strait. His canoe capsized on the way and he was stranded on a desert island with only a bottle of water and a tomahawk. For three days he was without food, except for a single oyster. A party of Korraregas, however, saw his fire and came to his rescue. Holding a grand corroboree in his honour, he was adopted into their tribe and exchanged names with an islander named Teepotti. The following morning, he was made a member of the Koolkalega tribe and exchanged names with an old man named Genetcha. Throughout his stay, as he preached a simple Gospel message, that was the name he was known by.[29]

Also in the Torres Strait around the same time period,

Thomas Huxley, the man who coined the word 'agnosticism' and who was known as *Darwin's Bulldog* for his advocacy of the theory of evolution, exchanged names with a young man named Do-outou.[30]

Many other examples exist of this rite.[31] However, let us move on from this survey. While it is by no means comprehensive, it is still sufficient to impart an overall understanding of what it meant to those native peoples who welcomed strangers into their midst.

English writers consistently remark on the custom of exchanging names as one of the highest friendship and deepest esteem[32] but, with only a few exceptions, fail to note its depth of spiritual meaning. They present it as charming but primitive. They do not identify it with one of the 'ancient paths' that Jeremiah laments has passed from common knowledge. No one recognises the Biblical overtones that go back millennia to the time when Abram exchanged names with El Shaddai and, in doing so, received a new name: Abraham.

By the eighteenth century, the concept of name covenant had all but disappeared within the sphere of Western ideas—with the limited exceptions of marriage and adoption. However European exposure to the idea continued through the writings that circulated about these journeys to the South Seas, to the American frontier, to the jungles of Africa, to the convict colony of New South Wales.

Perhaps the fading of the idea of name covenant was inevitable in the west. Covenant itself was no longer truly understood. It had become thoroughly confused with contract. The idea of incorporation into another family with all that that truly meant was too hard, too alien, too exotic and too unusual a notion. Western nations were intent on exploring the world to trade, colonise, exploit and profit—not to make brothers and sisters on the far side of the world.

2

Heart of My Own Heart

Be Thou my vision, O Lord of my heart;
Naught be all else to me, save that Thou art
Thou my best thought, by day or by night,
Waking or sleeping, Thy presence my light.

Be Thou my wisdom, and Thou my true Word;
I ever with Thee and Thou with me, Lord;
Thou my great Father, I Thy true son;
Thou in me dwelling, and I with Thee one.

Be Thou my armour, my sword for the fight;
Be Thou my dignity, Thou my delight;
Thou my soul's shelter, Thou my high tower:
Raise Thou me heavenward, O Power of my power.

Riches I heed not, nor man's empty praise,
Thou mine inheritance, now and always:
Thou and Thou only, first in my heart,
High King of heaven, my treasure Thou art.

High King of heaven, my victory won,
May I reach heaven's joys, O bright heaven's Sun!
Heart of my own heart, whatever befall,
Still be my vision, O ruler of all.

(attributed) Dallan Forgaill
(translated) Mary Byrne
(versified) Eleanor Hull

Sometime around the sixth century, Dallan Forgaill wrote this beautiful Irish lorica. A lorica is a warrior's protective breastplate and this song is meant to act as one in a spiritual sense. If it seems very peculiar that a song should act as a defensive shield, it's time to read Paul's advice in Ephesians 6:18 again at the end of his description of the Armour of God: *Pray in the Spirit at all times, with every kind of prayer and petition*. Prayer is the seventh and last piece of the divine panoply.

But this hymn is more than armour. It's a request for a name covenant.

Look at the first line: *Be thou my vision*. Dallan means *blind*. Here's the first hint: this druid-turned-monk didn't request God to *give* him sight; he asked God to *be* his sight.

Now look at the last line of the second verse: *Thou in me dwelling, and I with Thee one*. It is oneness that sets covenant apart from all other kinds of agreement. 'To be one' with another person is the distinguishing mark of a covenant with them—every other kind of pact falls short and drops into the category of contract or transaction.

Then there's—at least as far as I am concerned—the real clincher. The second line of verse three: *Be Thou my dignity, Thou my delight*. This is the original translation, which corresponds accurately to the ancient Gaelic. More recent versions of the hymn substitute: *Be Thou my armour and be Thou my might*.[33] Because we no longer know what a name covenant is, we fail to recognise the words that express how a name exchange brings us into a new family and, symbolised by the family mantle that we are gifted, comes honour, dignity and inheritance rights. Dallan

Forgaill's allusion to a mantle exchange—similar to those clothing and weapon exchanges across the Pacific—has been superseded by a reference to combat gear.

We lose out on a true understanding of the nature of spiritual warfare if we fail to realise that delighting in Him is far more important to Him than anything else. That unless we become heart of His own heart, we can win every spiritual battle but still effectively lose the greatest treasure of all: Jesus Himself.

The book of Revelation is the triumphant finale of Jesus' work of salvation. Ultimately it is about making all things new; and the first 'new' mentioned in John's vision of the end is about a new name. And it is likely to be no coincidence that this new name is associated with victory over the 'Nicolatians'. Dutch theologian, Willem Glashouwer, suggests that the reason the Nicolatians have been so notoriously difficult to identify is because they are not named after an early heretic at all. He suggests the word does not describe the teachings of a specific person called Nicolas, but instead is a descriptor which derives its meaning from the word 'nicolas', *victory of the people* or *conqueror of the people*.[34] For Glashouwer, the 'Nicolatians' were leaders who lorded it over others, conquering them in an emotional and spiritual sense— destroying, rather than encouraging, their contributions to the Body of Christ.

So the promised 'new name' is given to those who conquer the conquerors!

Culturally, the early Christians would have understood this perfectly.

The prophet Isaiah had promised that Jerusalem would be *called by a new name that the mouth of the Lord will give.* (Isaiah 62:2 ESV) Katheryn Pfisterer Darr comments that this unique phrasing is likely to be an allusion to the practice of cities being renamed by their conquerors as, for example, when Jerusalem—in a later age—became the colony of 'Aelia Capitolina'. For over half a millennium it was called by the family name of the Emperor Hadrian who razed the city in the second century.

Cities were also sometimes renamed to commemorate a significant event or when they were rebuilt. Renaming signifies a significant change in status or condition of the person receiving the new name. Darr points out that it may indicate coming under the subjugation of new authority. New throne-names were sometimes given to vassal-kings by their overlords.[35] And, of course, covenants, marriages and 'naturalisation' led to new names.[36]

But in the case of name covenants offered by God, it's not about conquering. Rather it's incredibly similar to those name exchanges discovered by Cook and Bligh, Lewis and Clark, Hanna and Douglas, Livingstone and Phillip, Gauguin and Stevenson. It's all about friendship.

Abraham was the first person to be called 'a friend of God'. And that special relationship came about through a name exchange. Abram had become part of the family of God through blood covenant. That had occurred when he was 86 years old—eleven years after he left Haran at God's direction. The relationship between Abram and his divine partner didn't begin with an instant adoption into God's family—rather it progressed through over a decade of acquaintanceship before that happened; before God covenanted with him for the first of four times.

Here in the twenty-first century, we don't even want to think about the numbers involved. Eleven years of being acquainted before the institution of blood covenant— *years*, not days or weeks. *Years*. Then another thirteen or fourteen years before the name covenant. Years *again*.

We want it all to be twinkling-of-an-eye immediate: we don't want our own faithfulness to have any impact on the length of time all this takes. We want the period of acquaintance, of blood covenant, name covenant, threshold covenant, salt covenant and covenant of peace to be bundled up into a lightning-swift split second. Yet God is interested in increasing depths of relationship, closeness and intimacy; and relationship takes *time*.

Here we have the essential difference between the name covenant that God offers us and the name exchanges that occurred in the last few centuries on the fringes of western civilisation: they don't occur on first acquaintance. And there's a very good reason why: if we are unfaithful to them, we call down destruction upon ourselves. Like James Cook in Hawaii, our ignorance can have fatal repercussions.

Abram was 99 years old when God appeared to him and announced, 'I am El Shaddai. Walk before Me and be holy.' Although El Shaddai is usually translated *God Almighty*, it would be more accurately rendered as *God the nurturer*. The root of 'shaddai' is *strong-breasted* and contains maternal imagery.

El Shaddai

In this exchange—the first *explicit* name covenant in Scripture—God reveals a new name for Himself. It's an implicit invitation for Abram to start using that name to call on the Lord.[37] God further offers him a part of His own name: He offers him the Hebrew letter 'hei', symbolic of pregnancy and fruitfulness. Abram becomes Abraham and Sarai becomes Sarah. And in so doing, they become one with God—again. This exchange expresses the thought: *'It is no longer "I" who live, but "we"'.*

We are 'heart of my own heart', as Dallan Forgaill said. We are two bodies sharing one heart—as Ibn Zabara said.[38] And we are 'two souls with but a single thought, two hearts that beat as one,' as Friedrich Halm wrote.[39]

This is a new level of oneness to the blood covenant God cut with Abram fourteen years previously. That covenant brought Abram into God's family as a son. This new covenant is about friendship. It reflects a maturation of the relationship; since not every son is a friend of his father. Moreover, sonship is a relationship that can never be lost. But friendship most certainly can.

When we are saved, we come into a blood covenant relationship with God. We become children of God. Just as we can never lose our status as a son or daughter of our earthly father, we can never lose our salvation; we can never forfeit our position as a child of God saved by the blood of His covenant. However, we can lose His friendship. And it's when we mock this offer of intimacy that life does an abrupt flip into fatality. There are some Scriptural instances of this we'll look at later.

For the moment, let's examine what God promised Abram in changing his name to Abraham. The usual translation of Abram is *exalted father*; of Abraham, *father of a multitude*; of Sarai, *princess* and of Sarah, *princess*.

These last two are very significant. There is absolutely no change in meaning from Sarai to Sarah. Both mean *princess*—the spelling makes no difference whatsoever. But spiritually, the letter 'h' when added to Sarai's name not only inserts the letter for pregnancy and fruitfulness into her identity, it adds a symbol for God. The Hebrews believed 'hei' to be shorthand for HaShem, The Name, itself a euphemistic shortening for the Name of God.

So the meaning of Sarah is more realistically *princess with God*. And if this is the case, what are the deeper spiritual connotations of Abraham?

Now when El Shaddai appeared to him, He announced, *'Behold, My covenant is with you and you shall be the father of many nations. No longer shall your name be called Abram, but your name shall be Abraham, for I have made you a father of many nations.'* (Genesis 15:4–5 NKJV)

As a result of this speech, almost all lexicons of Old Testament Hebrew declare Abraham to be derived from 'ab', *father*, and 'hamon', *multitude*. It therefore means *father of a multitude*. Now there's actually a problem with this. The issue is recognised by the Jewish Encyclopedia and by Arie Uittenbogaard at Abarim Publications. There's an R, 'rosh', unaccounted for.

The element at the end of Abram's new name is actually not 'hm' but 'rhm'—which doesn't mean *multitude* at all.

In fact, no one knows what the meaning is; it's unique. The element does not occur anywhere else in Scripture. The Jewish Encyclopedia goes so far as to state, 'The form "Abraham" yields no sense in Hebrew.'

But names are not solely about etymological meaning. Throughout all of my books, that's one of the thoughts I've repeated most often. Along with another: God is *not* primarily an etymologist. He's a poet. He doesn't ignore etymology entirely but He is far more interested in poetry and wordplay than our scientific age wants to admit.

Etymology gives us an inroad into the systematic analysis of a name's root meaning. But poetry is elusive and even defiant when attempts are made to dissect it in any formulaic, rationalistic way. Through the artistry and dreaming of nuances hidden within our names the Divine Wordsmith wrestles us towards the heart-of-my-own-heart space where He wants to commune with us.

Once we scrutinise the name Abraham in the light of possible poetry and wordplay, it's obvious that the true meaning matches God's announcement: *'Behold, My covenant is with you and you shall be the father of many nations.'*

The key words are *covenant*, *father* and *multitude*. The element 'brh' is embedded in the Hebrew of Abraham's name. And this element forms 'barah', the root of 'berith' meaning *to cut a covenant*. Thus in the overlap of *father*, 'ab', and 'hamon', *multitude*, is *covenant*, binding them both together.[40]

So, the scholarly statement that 'The form "Abraham" yields

no sense in Hebrew' is actually only true in etymological terms. God enfolds within the name Abraham both *father of a multitude* and *covenant-cutter* as well as the word 'Hebrew' itself—of whom Abraham was the first.[41]

This new name defined Abraham's new destiny. Name exchange says it's no longer 'me and me' but 'we'—and this covenant, covering all of Abraham's descendants forever—includes a divine promise that his line will last as long as the heavens and the earth do. In addition, they will be as numerous as the stars, as countless as the grains of sand on a seashore. Yes, Abraham will indeed be the *father* of a *multitude.*

Name covenants can adhere to several poetic patterns. Abraham is the first kind: the small tweak that makes a significant and subtle change in life direction for the person. Sarah is another example of this kind. As is Paul from Saul—however, surprising as this may be, it appears this name exchange was not with God but with a Roman consul! Another example of a small tweak is Joshua whose original name was Hoshea—and it's unclear whether this was a name exchange with God or simply a hypocorism[42] used by Moses (Numbers 13:16) which caught on across the entire assembly. Hoshea means *salvation* and Joshua means *salvation is in God,* so it could have been Moses' way of reminding his heroic young commander that it was far better to rely on God than on himself. On the other hand, it may well have been God's announcement through Moses of a name exchange: certainly Joshua—Yehoshua in Hebrew—contains the name of God whereas Hoshea does not.

Undoubtedly the most subtle of all name changes in Scripture is that of Phinehas, the grandson of Aaron. In a singular occasion in Numbers 25:11, 'Phinehas' is spelt with a small letter *yod*. At all other times, it has a regular size *yod*, symbolising *a strong right arm* or a *deed of might*.

This unusual spelling occurs as Phinehas leaves his post in front of the Tabernacle of the Lord, grabs a spear and heads off to kill a Simeonite prince and a Midianite princess. His action, violent and brutal as it is, stops the plague raging through the Israelite camp. As a result God gives him a covenant of peace, including a promise of an everlasting priesthood for his descendants. It may seem perverse of God to reward the very bloodshed He has just specifically told the Israelites to avoid in the Ten Commandments. However, as I have argued in *God's Priority*, I believe He granted favour because Phinehas deliberately entered the curse to bring healing to the people. In so doing, he became like the Messiah who would enter a curse for us to bring healing and peace.[43]

Since the covenant of peace seems to be the fifth in order—that is, we receive blood covenant first, then name covenant, then threshold, then salt, then peace— perhaps this subtle hint is meant to indicate that Phinehas was already friends with God. The covenant of peace was therefore in the right natural progression for him. Because if he had a name covenant, then he must have had threshold and salt too since, throughout Scripture, they occur together just six days after a name exchange. Of course there can be no absolute certainty that Phinehas had a name covenant with God but, to me, it seems extremely likely.[44]

The apostle Paul is an unequivocal example of name covenant. However it does not seem his was directly with God. Like those exchanges across the Pacific islands, his is one of several notable examples in Scripture of people covenanting with one another and receiving a new name.

It's a surprise to many people to realise Saul of Tarsus didn't immediately become Paul when, confronted by a vision of the risen Jesus, he fell down on the way to Damascus. It was well over a decade later before the transition happened. The exact timing is uncertain but, at some stage between eleven and seventeen years after his conversion—in the middle of his missionary journey to Cyprus—Saul appears to have agreed to a name covenant with the Roman consul, Sergius Paulus.[45]

Consequently, when he left Cyprus after performing his first recorded miracle, Saul had a new name. It's Paulus—which our English translations render as 'Paul'—and for the first time he begins to be pre-eminent in the partnership with Barnabas. Prior to this, Barnabas is always mentioned first, thereafter it's generally Paul first. In addition, prior to this, he's always called 'Saul'; thereafter it's uniformly 'Paul'.

Now the name Saul means *ask*, with overtones of *inquire*, *desire*, *pray*, *dedicate*, *question*, *consult a medium*.[46] It is related to *Sheol*, the Hebrew word for the nether regions of hell, the underworld, the grave, the place of exile.

Paul, on the other hand, is a Latin name meaning *small*. Now despite any covenant with a Roman consul, personally I really can't see Saul—a Hebrew of the Hebrews, of the tribe of Benjamin, a Pharisee, circumcised on the eighth day—

ignoring his heritage. I think 'Paul' has other overtones to the Hebrew mind. So let's suppose for a moment that 'Paul' sounds like a Hebrew word and thus has resonances and meaning across more than one language. The closest is 'palal', *to pray* or *to judge*. How wonderful! Here's an overlap with one of the meanings of Saul—*pray.* Here too is the single thread God has picked up for Paul to pursue for the rest of his life: *prayer and judgment.*

That judging began with Elymas, while he and Barnabas were on Cyprus. In fact, Cyprus was the homeland of Barnabas. His original name was Joseph and the apostles gave him the name 'Barnabas' which Luke translated for his Greek readers as *son of encouragement.* (Acts 4:36) That's a peculiar choice since 'barnabas' actually means *son of prophecy.* It seems Luke may have thought that Gentiles would read into *prophecy* such a mistaken idea he decided to offer 'paraklésis' as the closest equivalent that didn't have corrupted overtones. Certainly for the Greeks, prophecy meant foretelling the future, but for the Hebrews prophecy meant forthtelling a pattern—and so calling for repentance on the one hand and offering comfort on the other.

The word 'paraklésis' is the base of *paraclete*—a title of both Jesus and the Holy Spirit. In a courtroom setting, it means a legal advocate—a supporter who stands by your side to offer both counsel and comfort. In a military setting, it means the partner who has trained with you, knows your strengths and weaknesses, and who moves to stand back-to-back with you at the height of the battle. If you fall, your paraclete is the companion who steps to stand astride your body, protecting you. And who, when the battle is over, tends to your wounds.

Did Joseph, the Levite of Cyprus, receive a name covenant when the apostles called him 'Barnabas'? While there is no direct evidence this is the case, subtle hints point in that direction. He first appears at the end of the fourth chapter of Acts: *'Joseph, a Levite from Cyprus, whom the apostles called Barnabas (which means "son of encouragement"), sold a field he owned and brought the money and put it at the apostles' feet.'* (Acts 4:36–37 NIV)

Immediately after this brief introduction the narrative shifts to the story of Ananias and Sapphira. Like Barnabas, they too sell a field and put the money at the apostles' feet. But they've been deceitful about the deal and, when Simon Peter accuses Ananias of lying to the Holy Spirit, he drops dead. Not long after, so does Sapphira. This is a story about *threshold covenant*. Descriptors throughout the narrative—words like *feet at the door*, *conspire to test*, the series of choices—including the *choice* to repent and be truthful or to continue *lying*—suggest that the reason for the instant and fatal repercussions was threshold covenant violation. This is the pattern all the way back to Moses. It hasn't changed.

Now there can be no threshold covenant without a prior name covenant. There is no evidence of this in Acts 5 but it seems to me the introduction of Barnabas is meant to demonstrate this necessary prerequisite. Moreover, immediately before the mention of Barnabas are these words: *'All the believers were one in heart and mind,'* which is a way of saying they had covenanted together. And immediately after the Ananias and Sapphira story are these words: *'The apostles performed many signs and wonders among the people. And all the believers used to meet together in Solomon's Colonnade.'* (Acts 5:12 NIV)

This last word, *colonnade*, alludes to a covenant. Not for the Hebrews or Greeks but for the Romans.[47] The story is so shot through with covenant references that I believe 'Barnabas' was not a nickname but a name covenant. And why wouldn't it be? Jesus practised name covenant, so why wouldn't His disciples?

But if this is so, why make a riddle of it instead of spelling it out explicitly? This question, by its very nature, presupposes a western cultural expectation of forthright, unambiguous speech. That's not the way it's done in the East or Middle East.

Some Chinese friends of mine were explaining the problems they had encountered in translating a manuscript into Mandarin. Consider, they said, the meaning of the sentence, 'He took a photo of himself in front of Tiananmen Square.' There are many possible nuances but the writer was conveying a subtle message about the man's background—the same background as was in the photo: one of political privilege, prestige and influence. Such a man would never proclaim in a crass, assertive way: 'I'm a power-broker and deal-maker on the world's stage. I'm a high official who strides the corridors of power in the Chinese government.' He hints at his association with government in an allusive, even ambiguous way through the background in the photo.

For the majority of westerners, 'He took a photo of himself in front of Tiananmen Square' has none of these overtones. We want the message to be blunt and in-your-face, not indirect, subtle and inscrutable.

Yet the parables of Jesus are exactly that—indirect, subtle and inscrutable. The disciples find some almost impossible to understand, and have to ask for explanations. Sometimes I think it's a pity they didn't ask for more! Jesus could be so obscure in His speech that they didn't even realise He was talking about John the Baptist until He finally gave an unmistakeable hint.

Jesus is eastern—not western—in His thinking. So is Scripture. We have to look beyond the surface and pick up all the word clues that pertain to covenant, not just dismiss the possibility because there's no verse that says, 'Barnabas had a name covenant.'

Lois Tverberg points out that 'the prophets and other Biblical writers actually seemed to delight in pondering the nuances of their language. They often made wordplays based on a word's ambiguity, deliberately invoking multiple layers of a word's meaning.'[48]

Let's deal with the text as it is, not as we want it to be. '*It is the glory of God to conceal a matter; to search out a matter is the glory of kings.*' (Proverbs 25:2 NIV)

Now let's look at the time factor. Name covenant, as it occurred between God and Abraham, took place thirteen or fourteen years after the blood covenant between them. When the name covenant occurred between God and Jacob, it took place about twenty-one years after a covenant made with oil. This is a much rarer variety of covenant but take note of it—because it's certainly not the last of its kind.

Thirteen years for Abraham. Twenty-one years for Jacob. Bottom line: relationship takes *time.*

The more time spent together, the deeper the relationship. When we spare God just a few minutes a day, perhaps with an hour or so added on the weekend for a church service, we are drawing out the time until we're ready for a name covenant.

Now because relationship takes time, it should be no surprise that it took between eleven and seventeen years after Saul fell down, blinded by a vision of Christ, for his relationship with the Lord to have matured enough to go to the next level. At the *start* of his *first* missionary journey—note, it's the *start* and, note, it's the *first*—he accompanies Barnabas to Cyprus:

> *When they had gone through the whole island as far as Paphos, they came upon a certain magician, a Jewish false prophet named Bar-Jesus. He was with the proconsul, Sergius Paulus, a man of intelligence, who summoned Barnabas and Saul and sought to hear the word of God. But Elymas the magician (for that is the meaning of his name) opposed them, seeking to turn the proconsul away from the faith. But **Saul, who was also called Paul**, filled with the Holy Spirit, looked intently at him and said, 'You son of the devil, you enemy of all righteousness, full of all deceit and villainy, will you not stop making crooked the straight paths of the Lord? And now, behold, the hand of the Lord is upon you, and you will*

be blind and unable to see the sun for a time.'
Immediately mist and darkness fell upon him,
and he went about seeking people to lead him
by the hand. Then the proconsul believed,
when he saw what had occurred, for he was
astonished at the teaching of the Lord.

Acts 13:6–12 ESV

Here is the moment, emphasised in bold, when Saul becomes Paul. Look at what's happened: Saul is confronting his past self. He too had been temporarily blinded and had needed people to lead him by the hand; he too had tried to turn others away from the faith; he too had been an enemy of true righteousness; he too had been a Jewish false prophet, zealously proclaiming the Law in place of relationship with God.[49]

Now, outlandish as this may seem to many Christians today, no one knew about the *Sinner's Prayer* in the days of Paul and Barnabas. So how did the proconsul become a Christian? Unquestionably by repentance and baptism— and, of course, by covenant.

Saul and Barnabas probably had to explain 'covenant' to Sergius Paulus. And apparently he decided it'd be a good idea to exchange names with Saul. Thus Saul not only became Paulus but also part of the proconsul's family. Sergius Paulus may not have fully grasped the concept of name covenant but he would have been able to relate it to the Roman idea of patronage. Just a few decades after these events, the Jewish scholar Yosef ben Matityahu accepted Roman patronage and, assuming the family name of the emperor Titus Flavius Vespasianus, became Titus Flavius Josephus. We know him better as the historian Josephus.[50]

Is there any evidence Paul was actually adopted into the family of Sergius Paulus? Well, we know from Scripture that, when he left Cyprus, he headed for Pisidian Antioch. Although Scripture makes no mention of this, archaeological digs in Pisidian Antioch, dating back to 1912, have unearthed a stone slab with an inscription including the names 'Sergi.' and 'Paulus' on it—suggesting the proconsul in Cyprus sent his new brother in the faith straight to a family estate in present-day Turkey.

But why would the Holy Spirit prompt Saul to accept a name exchange with Sergius Paulus? Perhaps for a very practical reason: although Saul didn't yet know it, he was soon to see a man of Macedon in a dream who would plead with him: '*Come over to Macedonia and help us.*' (Acts 16:9 NIV) It would have been unwise to go to Greece with the name 'Saul'—where it meant *walk like a prostitute*.

God prepared the way so the name of the messenger would not get in the way of the Message.

The name change of Saul to Paul is the precursor to a new destiny. This is the purpose of name covenant: it is about the conception of a new calling. It is a summons into a new purpose in the kingdom of heaven; it's about a new friendship but it's also about a new inheritance; a changed future. This is true throughout Scripture—and it is also true in our lives today.

The earliest name exchange recorded in Scripture between two men, rather than man and God, is that between Joseph and Pharaoh. Again—in our era—we have to learn to spot the hints in order to realise there was a covenant between them. The biggest clue is in the opening chapter of Exodus: *'Now there arose up a new king over Egypt, who knew not Joseph.'* (Exodus 1:8 KJV)

The particular word used for *know* in this instance is 'yada', and it was often used as a way of expressing covenant. 'I know you,' meant 'I have covenanted with you.' Kings of the ancient world sometimes lamented betrayal of covenant by their vassals with an anguished cry: 'But I *know* you!'

So when Exodus 1:8 says that a new pharaoh came to power who did not *know* Joseph, it meant a lot more than simply one ruler died and another replaced him. It meant there was a change of dynasty. The family line of the original pharaoh who covenanted with Joseph was obligated to keep the covenant throughout all generations. Because, unlike contract, covenant has no end-date, no termination clause, no expiry. It involves the partners and their descendants *forever*. In the case of government, it involves the nations and its allies *forever*. To break a treaty is grave; to break a covenant brings down the full weight of the attendant curses.

But when a ruling house is overthrown and replaced by a new king on the throne, there is no obligation to keep the covenants agreed to by the previous dynasty. And this seems to be what happened in Egypt.

We actually happen to know what name Joseph received

in the exchange. Genesis 41:45 NIV informs us: *'Pharaoh gave Joseph the name Zaphenath-Paneah and gave him Asenath daughter of Potiphera, priest of On, to be his wife.'*

Now, of course, a name exchange—as we have seen both across various cultures and in the example of Abraham—involves men and women swapping all or part of their own name with another person. And in this statement about the name Pharaoh gave Joseph, we receive several important clues that should enable us, with just a tiny bit of detective work, to identify the actual Pharaoh involved.

Now covenants are about oneness but also about loyalty and devotion. This is why a warrior would have a covenant with his armour-bearer. On a purely practical level, many ancient rulers cut covenants rather than treaties because covenants bound the partners to an entirely different level of allegiance. So, any Pharaoh who took a slave straight from prison, elevating him in a single hour to a position second only to himself, would have been extremely naïve if he didn't extract some vows of personal loyalty. What better way than with covenant?

Pharaoh's covenant with Joseph makes perfect, practical sense. It seems that, in Zaphenath-Paneah, Pharaoh removed the dedication to Yahweh in Joseph's name—even though this was more than four centuries before God revealed Himself to Moses as the great I AM. Perhaps instinct told Pharaoh it was a divine name. This removes the 'jo' and leaves 'seph', apparently pronounced 'zaph'.

This gives us either 'enath' or 'paneah'—or both—as all or part of the Pharoah's name. Now, 'enath' is most likely since it also occurs in the name of Joseph's wife, Asenath, and perhaps her identity is recorded for this very reason: to point us in the right direction regarding Pharaoh.

So 'enath' is the most likely element swapped into Joseph's name from Pharaoh's. However, 'enath' is almost certainly derived from the name of the Canaanite war goddess, Anat. She first appears in Egypt during the period of the Hyksos invasion. The Hebrews spelled her name as Anath. Yes, Joseph's name lost the 'jo' for Yahweh and gained the name of a Canaanite goddess![51]

Now, is there any Pharaoh in the king lists of Egypt who has a name with a syllable like 'enath' or 'anat'? The only obvious ones are Anati Djedkare, Anat-her and Aperanat. Nothing is known about Anati Djedkare but Anat-her and Aperanat[52] appear to be father and son from the fifteenth or sixteenth dynasty. Some Egyptologists see Anat-her and Aperanat as Hyksos kings—Canaanite invaders famed for their introduction of horses and chariots in warfare. Others see them as vassals of the Hyksos. A seal belonging to Aperanat[53] has been found inscribed with *heqa khasut*, the Egyptian word for Hyksos.[54]

Now it makes sense that the Pharaoh who appointed Joseph was of Canaanite background, because this would not only explain why he made a covenant without a second thought but also why the covenant broke down centuries later. Joseph came from Canaan, the homeland of the Hyksos, so it was natural for such a ruler to appoint 'one of his own', a compatible thinker of similar background, rather than one of the subjugated locals whose loyalty might well be questionable. Furthermore when the Hyksos were kicked out of Egypt, any covenants made by their kings in previous centuries would no longer be operational. The obligation of mutual protection which existed under the covenant between Joseph and the Pharaoh—and which covered their families for generations—would no longer exist when the Hyksos were expelled.

Now I think we can actually identify the Pharaoh of this story as Aperanat. The reason involves the name of Joseph's second son, Ephraim. It's my personal belief that parents name their children for the unresolved issues of their family line.[55] And if Joseph did just that, then Ephraim's name points to the death of Joseph's mother, Rachel.

She died at Bethlehem Ephrathah, giving birth to his younger brother Benjamin. Now Ephraim and Ephrathah are closely linked names; and Hebrew 'ephra-' is basically the same as Egyptian 'apera-', the start of Aperanat's name. Ephraim's name is thus a truly brilliant fusion, commemorating both Joseph's mother as well as the ruler he had covenanted with. It's hard to get more diplomatic than that! Ephraim, meaning *doubly fruitful*, perhaps is a self-referential pun—telling the whole world of the time that it had more than one meaning.[56] Perhaps it even plays with Joseph's name, *God adds*, since doubling and adding are such closely related concepts.

Zaphenath-Paneah is a difficult name to translate and is variously rendered as Egyptian for *the one...appointed by God; God speaks, He lives; creator of life;*[57] *the one who furnishes the sustenance of the land,*[58] *the saviour speaks and lives, saviour of the universe, salvation of the age, sustainer of the life of the world,*[59] *governor of the district*

40

of the place of life,[60] *he who is called Ipiankhu, head of the sacred college, nourisher of the living one, master of the school of learning, governor of the region of Goshen,*[61] *a revealer of hidden things and an opener of things to come,*[62] *keeper of the treasury of the glorious rest.*[63]

Many of these interpretations rely on the thought that 'ath' at the end of the Zaphenath is really 'ankh', present in many Egyptian names and meaning *life*. I don't buy that explanation because I think this is part of a Canaanite name. The Jewish Encyclopedia gives the most extensive exposition of the name without arriving at any definitive answer. However, I think the difficulty is generally resolved by recognising the name is a mix of languages which has come about through name covenant.

Joseph rose to his position through his ability to interpret dreams. It therefore seems fitting that dreams were the provocation that so incensed his brothers they sold him into captivity. Yet dreams were also the means of his promotion.

Another famous dream interpreter of later times was Daniel who, like Joseph, was also a captive in a foreign land. Like Joseph, he was also exalted to a high position of trust, again second only to the rulers. And if Joseph's renaming does indeed signify a *keeper of the treasury*, then so too does Daniel's renaming.

Just as cities were sometimes renamed to indicate they were now occupied by a new ruling authority and just as new throne-names were sometimes given to vassal-kings by their overlords, then the princes of Judah in the time of Daniel who were being retrained to serve the Babylonians were given new names so they would forget the past. Daniel himself was renamed Belteshazzar, *keeper of the secret treasury of Bel*.

Just as Joseph seems to have been given a dedication to the goddess Anat within his new name, so Daniel was dedicated to the god, Bel the Confounder. Bel's name is to be found in 'Babel', the precursor of the city of Babylon.

Now Belteshazzar is fundamentally the same as Balthasar—a name that tradition assigns to one of the magi who visited Jesus. Furthermore, 'Casper' from the same tradition is Hebrew for *silver*, *treasure* or *treasury* as well.

There's perfectly logical sense to this tradition of Balthasar and Casper. The magi in the time of Jesus interpreted dreams, but so did Daniel five hundred years earlier; the magi survived an encounter with a homicidal heathen king and so did Daniel; the magi waited for clues from heaven about the birth of the Messiah. And so did Daniel. Who was, by the way, appointed chief of the magi twice in his own time.

Daniel had three friends: Hananiah, Mishael and Azariah. We know them better by the names the Babylonian officials gave them—names that were intended to supplant their old identities and rededicate their lives to the gods of Mesopotamia. Hananiah, Mishael and Azariah became Shadrach, Meshach and Abednego, *command of the moon god*, *shadow of the prince* and *servant of Nebo*.

The refusal of these courageous princes to bow to the Chaldean gods imposed on them did not begin at the fiery furnace—it began when they decided not to defile themselves with food from the king's table. 'Defile' suggests that these rich meats—these 'delicacies'—had first been offered to idols before reaching the king's banqueting hall. Eating them was therefore covenanting with the idols. The princes might not have been able to do much about what they were called by their captors but they resolved to draw a line in the sand about what they ate. Vegetables were safe: because vegetables didn't get sacrificed on altars to the gods.

Names, in and of themselves, are dedications—word signs and symbols of allegiance, faithfulness, commitment, loyalty, devotion. They are covenantal in nature.[64] They have positive and negative aspects—they encode choices. They spell out our calling and our destiny—not in any pre-determined sense but in terms of God's invitation to fulfil the works He prepared for us to complete before the foundation of the world.

He summons us into that vocation—but He does not compel us. Scripture shows us several instances where His gentle wooing was rejected. Along with the dire consequences that followed.

3

A Wrestle with Angels

A lot of people today don't believe in the power of words. And there are many different shades of disbelief that can occur. Some people think, for example, that the belief that naming something makes it real is part of an intellectual trap known as nominalism. David James says: 'Use a word like "peace" often enough and eventually it will seem that it has an independent existence. The next step is to make peace into a "thing" that can be examined in isolation: an intellectual error known as reification.'[65] He further comments that nominalism is related to the vice of positivism, the belief that something is only real if it can be measured.

This is one extreme—and certainly anyone who thinks like this will have problems with the medieval concept of Lady Peace and her sisters, Justice, Truth and Mercy. Moreover, they will have real problems in understanding the Biblical worldview where the words of a blessing or a curse constituted an active, living thing that could not be recalled. God, for example, promised Phinehas, grandson of Aaron, an everlasting priesthood and a covenant of peace. For some unknown reason, the line of the priesthood passed—for several generations—to that of his younger brother Ithamar, who was the father of Eli, who in turn was the father of Hophni and of another Phinehas. Hophni and the second Phinehas were so corrupt God pronounced a judgment on them. Look at how God confirms His covenantal vow in the first line and then proclaims a modification:

> 'I promised that members of your family would minister before Me forever... Far be it from Me! Those who honour Me I will honour, but those who despise Me will be disdained. The time is coming when I will cut short your strength and the strength of your priestly house, so that no one in it will reach old age, and you will see distress in My dwelling. Although good will be done to Israel, no one in your family line will ever reach old age. Every one of you that I do not cut off from serving at My altar I will spare only to destroy your sight and sap your strength, and all your descendants will die in the prime of life. And what happens to your two sons, Hophni and Phinehas, will be a sign to you—they will both die on the same day.'
>
> 1 Samuel 2:30–34 NIV

Now many people think that curses like this are the relic of a bygone age. And they consider anyone who does believe these words would come to pass just because an aggrieved person spoke it over an official as having thinking that belongs to the Dark Ages. It's primitive, archaic, superstitious.

Further along in the spectrum of thought about the power

of words are those people who do believe in curses, but consider they are all dealt with at the Cross. For these people, curses have no effect once we are born again because they are automatically dealt with by the blood of Jesus, without any need for personal or specific application.

Now covenants involve the power of words for both blessing and cursing. Covenants also, as previously mentioned, have no end-date, no termination clause, no expiry time. I believe that we are given the privilege of overcoming them through the power of the Cross and of the blood of Jesus. But I also believe that we need to flick the switch on that power in specific situations through words of repentance, renunciation, revocation and forgiveness. Our words in and of themselves do not provide any true and holy power—they don't enhance what Jesus has done for us, nor can they detract even the tiniest amount from it. All we can do is speak the words and invite Jesus to empower them to achieve God's will through them. From a human perspective, forgiveness and repentance are both impossible—but it is possible for us to declare an intention which we then ask Jesus to empower in us and achieve through us.

My experience is that, even reluctant words of forgiveness, empowered by Jesus are efficacious for miraculous healing. And my experience too is that, even casual words of repentance, empowered by Jesus are efficacious for new beginnings. I'm happy to hold an allegedly primitive view and believe in reification—to have faith that words create things that can be examined and even, in a sense, measured—because I've seen it happen too often. Both positively and negatively.

Name covenant is, as far as I can see, the most powerful driver of destiny in the Bible. Just a few tweaks of a word can create enormous change in individuals, propelling them to become the person they were always meant to be. Abram and Sarai, Phinehas and Saul: these are examples of people whose names underwent the smallest of changes and whose destinies then radically altered. The insertion of a letter, a change in size of a letter, a substitution of a letter—a tiny adjustment in their names meant a huge revolution in their destinies.

This kind of relatively minor fine-tuning or 'tweaking' is the first way God, the incomparable poet, transformed—and in fact still transforms—names and lives. The second way is by complete and radical overhaul.

Jacob: one of the most complete and radical name overhauls in the Scriptural record.

Jacob was the twin brother of Esau. Even before they were born, they struggled with each other. Jacob came out of the womb, clutching his brother's heel. And it was from this incident he received the name 'Jacob', *heel-grasper*— also with the sense of *supplanter*, *deceiver* and *usurper*. In Hebrew, *heel* is also the word for *if*, the definitive word that sits in the front of our thoughts whenever choices arise in life. The name Jacob basically suggests someone who cynically manipulates the options presented to him to his own advantage.

Throughout his life, Jacob lived up to his name: he coerced Esau into giving up his birthright and he deceived his father so he could receive the blessing of the firstborn. He also deceived his uncle, adding to his own flocks at Laban's expense by practising primitive fertility magic.

Mind you, practised swindler as Jacob was, he could have taken lessons from his uncle, an arch-deceiver who out-foxed him continually regarding his wages, his hire conditions and even his marriage partner! As for Esau, there's no question he despised his birthright but that doesn't excuse Jacob's culpability. Esau had come in from, exhausted and hungry. Smelling Jacob's cooking, he said: *"'Please let me have a swallow of that red stuff there, for I am famished." Therefore his name was called Edom.'* (Genesis 25:30 NAS)

Esau traded with Jacob: his *birthright* for some *red*. The actual text doesn't contain the word 'stew' or 'pottage' or 'stuff'—just *red*. Esau's name changes at this moment, as if there's covenant involved. He becomes 'Red', the meaning of Edom. And perhaps there's indeed a covenant in play here, because a name exchange brings with it an introduction to a new family and an entitlement to an inheritance—or a birthright—within that family. When Jonathan covenanted with David, he gave up the inheritance he could have expected as the eldest son of Saul: that of the throne. He confirmed the anointing of David as the next king.

'Jacob I loved, but Esau I hated,' the Lord declares in Malachi 1:2 ESV. Paul quotes this in Romans 9:13. Esau despised his birthright—his identity and destiny—two elements that are sealed in a name. He therefore despised the covenant over the name his parents had given him.

Covenant is incredibly important to God. We see that when we contrast David and Saul. David—an adulterer, a murderer, a negligent father whose indifference to the rape of his daughter by her half-brother set a catastrophic chain of events into motion, a liar whose trickery brings about the death of all the priests of Nob, a deceiver who pretended to serve his Philistine enemies—was a man after God's own heart!

Yet Saul is not. Saul's sins are great, yes, but David is not a man of immaculate integrity. Joab was so enraged about the men who were sacrificed to make Uriah's death look like a casualty of war that he called for shame to contend with David and compared him to Abimelech, the man who slaughtered seventy of his kinsmen on a single stone in order to rule Israel.

So why was David favoured and Saul not? Why was Esau hated and Jacob not? In the end, I believe it's because David and Jacob kept covenant, while Saul and Esau treated it lightly. God takes covenant-keeping seriously and detests covenant-breaking. Whenever a harsh, instant response on God's part occurs in Scripture, look for covenant violation—not of blood covenant, because God takes those curses on Himself, but of name or threshold covenants.

Jacob was the grandson of Abraham—a man who had four covenants with God. Blood, name, threshold, salt. It's my belief he didn't ever get the fifth covenant, that of peace, because he failed to pass the test God set him after coming to visit him while on His way to Sodom. Yes, I know, I know. So many commentators, both Christian and Jewish, say that Abraham was set ten divine tests during his life and he passed them all. They might disagree about what those ten tests were, but they don't disagree about the number. Gentlemen, with respect, I have to inform you—from a woman's point of view, putting your wife at risk in a foreign country because you don't trust God to protect you, does *not* constitute passing a test. Asking her to conceal the true relationship between you—that you are husband and wife—does not bespeak overwhelming faith in God as your covenant defender.

Abram deceived Pharaoh about Sarai, and disasters struck Egypt. Pharaoh's anguish in realising the cause of his people's affliction is reflected in words that were previously used by God in Eden: '*What have you done?*' (Genesis 12:18 NIV)

Twenty-five years and four divine covenants later, God gives Abraham a chance to redo the same test. You'd think that in that time Abraham would have learned that God is a faithful, unfaltering covenant-keeper. But no. In Gerar, in the kingdom where Abimelech rules, he re-enacts exactly the same deceit and asks Sarah to repeat the half-true story she is his sister. He fails again.

The unresolved issue in Abraham's life is deceit. Despite his incredible faith in other circumstances, this is the one thing he can't trust God with—his own safety if he takes his wife to a foreign land. The test passes down to Isaac who has an opportunity to pass an eerily similar test, also in the land of Gerar. But Isaac follows his father's example. The unresolved family issue—deceit—is now so prominent that Isaac and Rebekah name their son for it: Jacob, *deceiver*.

Name is the fuse of identity, the power source propelling

us into our destiny. Jacob is the one called to deal with the deceit in his family line but, to begin with, he simply adds to the mess. He uses the skin of a goat to deceive his father in order to gain the blessing of the firstborn—many years later he will reap what he sown and a goat will be used to deceive him when the bloodied coat of his favourite son is brought to him.

This aspect of naming—of declaring the family's unresolved spiritual issues, along with proclaiming the one chosen to solve those issues—finds expression in the Māori practice of breathing a secret name into the fontanelle of a newborn child. A grandfather may whisper, 'Murderer,' or 'Rapist' or something similar, assigning the child a role of 'utu', *payback*, involving that specific name.

But God wants to liberate such children from the weight of the burden imposed on them, just as He wanted to liberate Jacob from the deceit dominating his line. The fact is, God had wanted all along for Abraham to pass the test concerning his wife, Sarah. That's why He gave him two chances! And why He placed Isaac in the same scenario—offering a third chance.

In many respects, we can see that *deceiver* should never have been Jacob's name—he should always have been 'Israel', a male variant of the feminine 'Sarah', after his grandmother!

Jacob encountered the angel who called him 'Israel', *contender with God* or *prince with God*, at the ford of Jabbok. There they wrestled until daybreak. In Hebrew, Jabbok is Yabboq and Jacob is Ya'aqob. Ya'aqob at Yabboq engaged in a ye'abeq, *wrestle*, that resulted in his leg being yaqa'—'out of joint'.

There's a lot of playful poetry there.[66] And, as God the poet—the consummate Wordsmith—composes the poem of our lives, He sometimes has to write us into corners to compel us to deal with our unresolved issues. For some of us, just as they were for Jacob, those problems are declared in and through our names.

The covenantal imagery in the story of Jacob forms a strong background to the story of his acquisition of a new name. And it's threshold covenant that is emphasised there—as is appropriate since name and threshold covenant properly occur in the same week, six days apart. This threshold covenant setting includes a camp of angels (Genesis 32:1), the crossing of a boundary stream (Genesis 32:22), the sacrificial gift (Genesis 32:13–15). It is unclear whether a name exchange occurred—though it's clear Jacob wanted it. The angel, on being quizzed about his identity, inquires, '*Why do you ask my name?*' and then blesses Jacob. Perhaps the blessing included an unrevealed name.[67] Particularly since 'mah' the word for *why* or *what* is going to come up again in a very significant context involving a name offering.

But that involves refusing a name covenant—so let's return to it later, after examining other examples of radical name overhaul.

Almost as soon as Simon met Jesus, he was told he would be one day called 'Cephas'. (John 1:42) But in fact, that renaming doesn't happen for almost exactly another two years.[68] It occurred when Jesus had taken His disciples up north to a notorious centre of idolatry. They had gone to Caesarea

Philippi, on the south-western slopes of Mount Hermon.

Around sixty years previously, Mark Antony had executed the local ruler for supporting the Persians against the Romans. Dividing the land into quarters, he had given a portion to his lover, Cleopatra, queen of Egypt. She had then proceeded to lease the extensive territory she'd been gifted to the heir of the executed ruler! When she died, he resumed the titles of his predecessor, 'tetrarch and high priest'. However, on his death, they were then bestowed by Rome upon Herod the Great. The territory included Paneas, now called Banias, which got its name from a temple precinct dedicated to the rustic god Pan.[69] This Greek cultic shrine specialised in worshipping the god of panic and included a cave with gushing spring.[70] Here, it was said, were the 'Gates of Hell' and into this cave, sacrificial offerings—including bound and drugged humans—were thrown.

After Herod's death, this area—the Paneion—was inherited by his son, Philip, whose mother was Cleopatra of Jerusalem. Nothing is known about this mysterious woman other than her name; she may indeed be identical with Cleopatra of Egypt. Herod had a complex relationship with that queen—he had to lease the lush oasis of Jericho from her after Mark Antony gave it to her as another gift and he had to share with her in the bitumen trade of the Dead Sea.[71]

Whether the region around Paneas passed from mother to son is unclear. What is clear is that, about thirty years before[72] Jesus took His disciples there, Philip renamed it Caesarea Philippi, the name immortalised in the gospels as the place where Simon declares Jesus to be the Messiah.

The shrine to Pan, which was set up in the time of Alexander the Great, was often mistaken in ancient writings for the sanctuary of Dan. Archaeological digs, however, locate Dan about six kilometres away.[73] Dan was one of the places of pilgrimage set up in opposition to the temple in Jerusalem, after the split in the kingdom in the time of David's grandson. Ten tribes rebelled against Rehoboam, set up their own rival monarchy—in the Northern Kingdom of Israel—and worshipped golden calves. One was here at Dan and another was at Bethel.

The entire region around Mount Hermon was dotted with temples—about twenty of them from the Roman era alone. There were also sanctuaries going much further back—the book of Joshua mentions 'Baal Gad' in the Valley of Lebanon below Mount Hermon—the name indicating worship of the 'Lord of Luck' or 'God of Fortune', perhaps ~p.129~ even with the nuance, 'God of Fortune in Battle'.

~→ Yahushua was later transfigured here~

This was seriously serious pagan territory. Moreover it was all in the shadow of Mount Hermon—the 'forever ~(p.69)~ accursed' mountain where, according to the Book of Enoch, a group of fallen angels descended from the heavens and made a pact to take human wives. This was also the 'mount of assembly' of the Canaanite pantheon, where the seventy sons of their supreme god had a palatial abode.

In front of Pan's grotto—with its reputed entrance to hell—Jesus began a remarkable conversation that included a name exchange. Read carefully and you'll see Simon give Jesus a title and Jesus give him a new name.

Now when Jesus came into the district of Caesarea Philippi, He asked His disciples, 'Who do people say that the Son of Man is?'

And they said, 'Some say John the Baptist, others say Elijah, and others Jeremiah or one of the prophets.'

He said to them, 'But who do you say that I am?'

Simon Peter replied, 'You are the Christ, the Son of the living God.'

And Jesus answered him, 'Blessed are you, Simon Bar-Jonah! For flesh and blood has not revealed this to you, but My Father who is in heaven. And I tell you, you are Peter, and on this rock I will build My church, and the gates of hell shall not prevail against it. I will give you the keys of the kingdom of heaven, and whatever you bind on earth shall be bound in heaven, and whatever you loose on earth shall be loosed in heaven.'

Then He strictly charged the disciples to tell no one that He was the Christ.

Matthew 16:13–20 ESV

Simon gives Jesus the title 'Messiah' and Jesus gives him the name Cephas—which is the Hebrew equivalent of the Greek 'Petros'. In English, we say 'Peter' and translate it as *rock*. But it isn't any ordinary rock. The original name 'Cephas' gives us the clue. This is the threshold stone, the cornerstone, which a guest has to pass over in order to come into covenant with a host.

Jesus—the Chief Cornerstone—bestows on Simon one of His own names.

A name covenant in Scripture requires two things: first, the exchange of names—which, when it is with God, involves a revelation by the Holy Spirit of a hitherto unknown name so that, for example, Abram can call God 'El Shaddai' and Simon can call Jesus 'Messiah'. Secondly, the name covenant requires a threshold covenant in—ideally—a six-day period.

Both Matthew and Mark mention[74] that six days after Simon makes this confession of faith and becomes Cephas—or Peter—he accompanies Jesus, along with James and John, up a high mountain. There Jesus is transfigured.

Luke says that it's *about* eight days.[75]

For Matthew and Mark, the writers of Hebrew background, it's necessary to get the number exactly right because their audience will pick up on the significance of the six days. But Luke, writing for a Gentile audience, doesn't need to be so accurate. The Greeks and Romans aren't going to recognise the implications of 'six days' in relation to naming within the creation story.[76] And none of them would have known what modern medicine has revealed—that, unless a fertilised egg is implanted in the womb within six days, it will naturally abort. Just so, unless a Spirit-breathed name is ratified by a threshold covenant within—ideally—six days, then the destiny encoded in that name will miscarry.

Jesus speaks into Simon's confession of faith, declaring it as the threshold stone on which the church will be built. This moment, on the day of Yom Kippur, is that flashing instant of 'conception' for the church. Six days later, at the start of the Feast of Sukkot, God speaks during the Transfiguration confirming and 'implanting'—in, as Dwight Pryor points out, the words of a midwife—so that the conception is secure. Some eight and a half months later, at the Feast of Pentecost, the church is 'born'.

Ultimately, for the Jews, name was always about conception. This incident of Jesus and Simon exchanging names is no exception. In this instance, however, the conception extends beyond the individual to the body of believers as a church. Jesus, as He speaks His church into existence, is also issuing a challenge to the spirit world and to the 'genii loci', *the spirits of the place*.

We can see in His words a variety of references to the spiritual deposits laid down in the landscape through its history: subtle allusions to Cleopatra and to Dan, as well as the blatant mention of the entrance to Hades at Pan's Grotto.

Gates of hell: not only is this a direct reference to the entry to the underworld at the shrine, it's a double entendre. In Hebrew, 'gates' were synonymous with judges because that is where they sat. And the word for *judge* is Dan! As for Cleopatra, her name is obliquely referenced in the phrase, 'keys to the kingdom'. Cleopatra is generally said to mean *glory of the father* or *glory of the fatherland*.

However, it can also mean *keys of the fatherland*.[77]

Jesus is speaking to the land and healing its history. Those words, '*on this rock I will build My church, and the gates of hell shall not prevail against it*', are going to be very significant just a few short years down the track. As just mentioned, 'gates' was so evocative of *judges* and *judgment* that the terms were virtually interchangeable. And while 'hell' might have been Hades in Greek, in Hebrew it was Sheol, a word directly related to the name Saul.

The road to Damascus led through here. Saul of Tarsus would have come this way as he headed north with letters from the high priest to seize and imprison the followers of Jesus. Today, those letters would be arrest warrants or legal injunctions.

'The judgments of Saul shall not prevail against My church,' is one sense of what Jesus said, just before He mentioned legal injunctions. Because that's exactly what Jesus is talking about when He used the phrase 'bind and loose': legal injunctions both in the natural world and the spiritual. He was speaking about the very thing Saul was carrying with him as he expanded his mission to destroy the church of God: letters of authority which gave him an official right to detain and incarcerate anyone who could be considered a Christian. And more than that, Jesus was speaking into Saul's name and negating those legal papers several years in advance of Saul's visit to this very region.

Jesus left His own spiritual deposit in this territory to protect His church—not just at its moment of conception but for the time when it would be a toddler under serious threat.

It's worth repeating: ultimately, for the Jews, name was always about conception. When we are conceived, God breathes into each of us a soul just as He did for the first man, Adam. And because the word for *breath*, 'nashamah', has an embedded 'shem', *name*, Jewish sages consider that this indicates God creates our souls through naming. In a whisper of love, He breathes a name into us, defining both our identity and our destiny.

> *And the Lord God formed man of the dust of the ground, and breathed into his nostrils the breath [nashamah] of life; and man became a living soul.*
>
> Genesis 2:7 KJV

A word is the medium by which we are given life. A name infuses a soul into us—God speaks each of us individually into being, just as He created light through a word. '*And God said, "Let there be light," and there was light.*' (Genesis 1:3 NIV) In Hebrew, God simply tells light to be: '*Be, light!*' is what the text says. That very first word He says—the opening word of creation as recorded by Scripture—is simply God's name.[78]

How on earth, you might wonder, does God's name relate to the word *be*? Isn't it Yahweh, *I AM*? Now, with absolutely no apology for this excursion into the quirky nature of English grammar, let's note how the irregular verb *to be* is conjugated. It goes like this: I am, you are, he is, she is, it is, we are... and so on. Significantly, the first person singular of *to be* is 'I am'—recognisably the name of God.

In Hebrew, *be* is 'hayah'. This same word 'hayah' is used in Exodus 3:14 when God calls Himself 'I am'. At this point, we need to clear up a critical misconception about God's name. If I'd known this, I could have saved myself a decade of anguish in my relationship with God. His name is *not* Yahweh. Let me repeat that. God's name is *not* Yahweh. He never self-revealed using the name Yahweh. The Hebrew people, in their quest to keep the name of God holy and inviolate, consistently used Yahweh to avoid His actual name.

'Yahweh', although it is repeatedly used in Scripture in places other than Exodus 3:14, is actually one step removed from the sacred name. It is *not* what God told Moses. Yahweh means *He Is Who He Is*. If you look back two paragraphs to the conjugation of the verb, *to be*, you'll discover that this is a grammatical shift from first person singular to third person singular: from 'I am' to 'he is'.

God, however, when He was talking to Moses at the burning bush called Himself 'Ehyeh' or 'Hayah'. And this is the name that means *I Am Who I Am*.

Now when God reveals a new name for Himself—as, for example, El Shaddai to Abram or Messiah to Simon—it's a name covenant He's offering. The most important principle of name covenants with God is here: they will partake of His own name. With the exchange comes a new calling and destiny, and along with that comes the threshold covenant and its invitation to friendship.

So where does Moses receive a new name? Well, he doesn't. Not because God didn't offer it, but because Moses refused to accept the offer. The name exchange that God proposed is not at all obvious in English, but in

Hebrew it's to be found in one of those fun, tweaky puns God is so fond of when He's wordsmithing.

He repeatedly asks Moses, '*What is it...?*' in reference to the things in his hand. Now Moses is 'Moseh' in Hebrew and '*What is it...?*' is 'mazeh'. The 'mazeh' in his hand is, by turns, a staff, a snake and a leprous condition. Much later the *what-is-it* will be the manna that falls each day to sustain the people in the wilderness. But for the moment, it is Moses' trusty, reliable staff which has just morphed into a snake.[79]

> *Moses answered: "What if they do not believe me or listen to me and say, 'The Lord did not appear to you?'"*
>
> *Then the Lord said to him, "What is that in your hand?" "A staff," he replied.*
>
> *The Lord said, "Throw it on the ground." Moses threw it on the ground and it became a snake.'*
>
> Exodus 4:1–3 NIV

Now Moses' staff wasn't just the stick he leaned on—it also represented his vocation and his security. It announced to the world that he was a shepherd. But it was also the way he protected the flock. As well as himself. So when God told him to throw it down, he was asking Moses to let go of the identity and sanctuary he'd created for himself.

Because: the staff also symbolised ideal qualifications for God's call. The staff, as the symbol of a desert shepherd, indicates Moses can herd sheep and keep them alive in a dangerous wilderness. He knows the weather signs, the location of wells and oases, the hostile wildlife—snakes, scorpions, jackals and foxes.

But that shape-change of his staff to a serpent says something else. In the centre of a Pharaoh's double crown sits a cobra—the emblem of the royal house. The appearance of the serpent says this: Moses, you have a background and an upbringing that will enable you to negotiate and navigate through the protocols of the Egyptian court.

Moses says 'no' to God's offer of a name exchange. And he backs it up with another 'no'. And another. And another. And another. And to make it absolutely clear to God that 'no' means 'no', a few days later he undertakes a threshold covenant with an enemy of God. This forfeits all his protection from God as his covenant defender. In fact, it sets God implacably against him:

> On the way to Egypt, at a place where Moses and his family had stopped for the night, the Lord confronted him and was about to kill him. But Moses' wife, Zipporah, took a flint knife and circumcised her son. She touched his feet with the foreskin and said, "Now you are a bridegroom of blood to me." (When she said "a bridegroom of blood," she was referring to the circumcision.) After that, the Lord left him alone.
>
> Exodus 4: 24–26 NLT

The whole incident is summarised in just three verses— certainly some of the most mysterious in all Scripture. To understand the significance of what transpires here, we have to realise Moses had just repeatedly turned God's invitation to a name covenant. Since name and threshold covenants go together, he's thumbed his nose at that too. Still he has headed off for Egypt but somewhere en route, he's taken lodging. In those days—and for that matter, still today, in Bedouin encampments—stepping over a threshold is about host and guest covenanting together.

Perhaps Moses thought he was far enough away from the mountain of the Lord to escape Him and seek protection with another god. It's clear something like that has happened because the unusual Hebrew word for *lodging place*, 'malon',[80] seems to be a combination of 'maal', *act treacherously*, and 'lun', *lodging*.

Because of Moses' act of betrayal, God tries to kill him.

None of this comes across in the English translation. And because we are unaware of the cultural nuances— that in accepting hospitality and, in passing through the doorway, Moses came into covenant relationship with the host—we're at a loss to understand the situation. This act of accepting lodging bears no resemblance to our modern way of doing things—it's not a simple monetary transaction. It's a covenant—a relationship whose primary purpose is 'oneness'.

In stepping over the threshold into the lodging, Moses acted treacherously—so this wasn't any ordinary wayside inn he'd entered. This shelter from the wind, sun and sand was probably a remote shrine to a desert god. And, in becoming one with that god, Moses would have been defiled and therefore tempted to bring the people out of Egypt to worship it, not the Lord of the Burning Bush.

God acted abruptly and harshly because Moses was threatening to derail the Exodus before it even happened. Moses' wife, Zipporah, saved his life. She remembered the 'sign' of the covenant. She remembered what Moses has forgotten. She remembered that El Shaddai—who has just revealed Himself as 'I AM'—long ago asked Abraham to circumcise all the males as a symbol of their dedication to Him. And she remembered that this hasn't happened for all the males in the room. So she took decisive action.

She performed a circumcision—whether it was on Moses himself or whether it was on their son, Gershom, is unclear in the original text. But with this reaffirmation of covenant, God ceased His attack.

This reaffirmation of covenant with the Lord, with all its implications of renunciation of other gods, revocation of unholy vows, forgiveness and repentance, is a key aspect of dealing with our agreements with the powers of darkness.

Refusing a name covenant when God offers one is serious. It's also refusing a threshold covenant, a salt covenant and a covenant of peace. Really super serious.

But, to make it far worse, if God makes you such an offer and you then turn around and make a threshold covenant with His enemy, you're indulging in an unbelievable level of defiance. And ultimately, because name covenant is about an offer of friendship, it's also an insane level of betrayal.

When God offers us a name covenant, it's not humility to refuse the call. And if Moses can make this tragic mistake,[81] so can we.

*Now Moses used to take the tent and pitch it outside the camp, far off from the camp, and he called it the tent of meeting. And everyone who sought the Lord would go out to the tent of meeting, which was outside the camp. Whenever Moses went out to the tent, all the people would rise up, and each would stand at his tent door, and watch Moses until he had **gone into** the tent. When Moses **entered** the tent, the pillar of cloud would descend and **stand at the entrance** of the tent, and the Lord would speak with Moses. And when all the people saw the pillar of cloud standing at the entrance of the tent, all the people would rise up and worship, each at his tent door. Thus the Lord used to speak to Moses face to face, as a man speaks to his friend.*

Exodus 33:7–11 ESV

It would appear from this passage that Moses eventually became God's friend. But I'm not convinced the Hebrew is completely unambiguous on this score. There's something terribly wrong in the description: God is standing at the entrance to the tent speaking to Moses from the outside. To be sure a threshold covenant is in operation we'd need to know God *entered* the tent. That is by no means certain. Yes, certainly He's speaking with Moses **as with** a friend, but that's not quite the same as saying 'the Lord used to speak with His friend Moses, face to face.'[82]

Certainly an argument can be made to the contrary here

but, for me, the defining incident showing a name covenant never happened for Moses occurred towards the end of his life. For the best part of forty years, manna (*'what is it?'*) rained down daily. It had not only provided the food of angels for the people of Israel but it had relentlessly reminded Moses that mazeh (*'what is it?'*) was the fine-tune God wanted for his name.

But somehow it was easier to get Moses out of Egypt than it was to get Egypt out of Moses. He clung to the name Pharaoh's daughter gave him, resisting all God's reminders to make the smallest of sound changes towards a Hebrew name.

God, it seems, finally compromised. When Moses wanted to provide water for the people, God told him to draw water from a rock by speaking to it. Now, *drawn from the water* is the meaning of the Egyptian name Moses. God gave him yet another chance to accept a small tweak for his name. But he refused. And, once again, it was a very definite 'no'. Moses struck the rock.

And God basically said: 'Enough!' He denied Moses and Aaron permission to enter the Promised Land. For apparently the most minor of infractions, the two leaders were barred from the land of milk and honey that had been the object of their dreams.

But it's not as minor as it seems. The Hebrew word used for *striking* has the connotation of *refusing threshold covenant*. In front of the assembly, Moses made a very public declaration—he disobeyed God concerning the symbolism of his name, he therefore rejected God's calling with regard to that name, and thus he refused threshold covenant as well. As leader of the assembly, his actions were tantamount to refusing covenant on behalf of the people. God, in His mercy, actually confined that refusal to Moses and Aaron—otherwise, the people would have had to enter the Promised Land without a divine covenant defender.

Years before, God had offered a name covenant to the people of a previous generation. As usual, He revealed a new name for Himself. Here is the passage where it's hidden—it's so unusual a name, you may never have heard of it before:

> 'I am going to send an angel before you to protect you on the way and bring you to the place I have prepared. Be attentive to him and listen to him. Do not defy him, because he will not forgive your acts of rebellion, for My name is in him. But if you will carefully obey him and do everything I say, then I will be an enemy to your enemies and a foe to your foes.'
>
> Exodus 23:20–22 CSB

God then outlines His covenant promises, and warns of the curses which will fall on the people by detailing the consequences of not keeping covenant. Immediately after this, in the following chapter, Moses reads out the scroll of the agreement and all the people respond they will obey the Lord implicitly. Then Moses takes the blood of sacrifice and pours half on the altar and sprinkles the people with the other half.

It looks like a blood covenant—but it's not. It's a name covenant. Two things give this away: one, the revelation of a hitherto unknown divine name and, two, the fact that Moses, Aaron, Nadab, Abihu and seventy of Israel's elders were invited to dine with God. They were invited to threshold covenant; a fact made clear when Moses is summoned back after the banquet and has to wait in the cloud for *six* days. This is the standard time-frame between a name covenant and its 'implantation' as a threshold covenant.

Now you may be wondering what this unusual name is and where it's concealed. It's quite obvious—it's in the phrase, 'My name is in him.' In Hebrew, this is a double entendre. The word for *in him* is 'qareb'. It's a rhyme for 'cherub', possibly identifying the nature of the angel. It's also a rhyme for 'Horeb', one of the names for the mountain where this conversation is occurring. However, most importantly, its ancient spelling is identical to the word, 'qereb', *war*.

'My name is war.'

This angel had one purpose, and only one: war. If the people obeyed, it would war against their enemies. But if they failed to follow its commands, it would war against them.[83]

⁂

'My name is *in him*.'

'My name is *war*.'

'The Lord is a man of war; the Lord is His name.' (Exodus 15:3 ESV)

God is also a master of paradox. He's a Lord of perfect

justice and, contrariwise, of perfect mercy. He's a God of total truth but He allowed a deceiving spirit to do His bidding.[84] So, of course, because the Lord is also the Prince of Peace, there's another name covenant recorded in Scripture where He reveals the name, *peace*, for the first time.

This name covenant again involves an angel. In fact, one of the signature marks of the six-day period when both the name and threshold covenants take place is the presence of angels. It was so for Abram when, a few days after receiving the new name Abraham, God turned up with two angels for a threshold covenant. It was also so for Jacob who wrestled with an angel from a nearby angelic encampment and received a new name. It was so for Moses, even though he rejected the offer of a name covenant, when an angel of the Lord appeared to him in a burning bush. It was so for the people of Israel when the conditions for the help of an angel named War were outlined. And it was so for Gideon to whom God reveals his name: '*The Lord is peace.*'

The story of Gideon in fact begins with the appearance of the angel:

> *Now the angel of the Lord came and sat under the terebinth at Ophrah, which belonged to Joash the Abiezrite, while his son Gideon was beating out wheat in the winepress to hide it from the Midianites. And the angel of the Lord appeared to him and said to him, 'The Lord is with you, O mighty man of valour.' And Gideon said to him, 'Please, my lord, if the Lord is with*

us, why then has all this happened to us?'

Judges 6:11–13 ESV

After expressing a fair bit of doubt about the 'mighty man of valour' tag he's been given, Gideon offers a gift which is consumed in fire as the angel disappears. Gideon, shocked, says:

> *'Alas, O Lord God! For now I have seen the angel of the Lord face to face.' But the Lord said to him, 'Peace be to you. Do not fear; you shall not die.' Then Gideon built an altar there to the Lord and called it, The Lord Is Peace. To this day it still stands at Ophrah...*

Judges 6:22–24 ESV

Now we have gathered all the pieces and clues, let's see what is happening in this name exchange. In Hebrew, the words translated 'mighty man of valour' are actually *army strong man*. Now, while Gideon means *hewer* or *axeman*, the first syllable of his name is the word for *troop*, *army* or *fortune*. God isn't changing Gideon's name as He did Jacob's or Abram's or Simon's—essentially, He's just redefining and redirecting it to emphasise that initial syllable.

Sometimes this is what God will do for us: He won't change our name; He'll simply tell us to focus on a specific part of it. The story of Gideon reveals another aspect of name covenant, however: we don't lose our original name and we still have to deal with it. Gideon's first action in his new calling is as an *axeman*, not as an *army leader*. He chops down his father's idolatrous Asherah pole in accordance with God's instructions:

> *That same night the Lord said to him, '...Tear*
> *down your father's altar to Baal and cut*
> *down the Asherah pole beside it. Then build a*
> *proper kind of altar to the Lord your God on*
> *the top of this height.'*

Judges 6:25–26 NIV

God might be redefining Gideon's name but He's not erasing the past meaning. We see a similar thing when Jesus addresses Peter at the Last Supper: *'Simon, Simon, Satan has asked to sift each of you like wheat.'* It's not as Cephas or Peter he's addressed—the name he's been sporting for nearly seven months—but as 'Simon'. Jesus is telling him that Simon is going to be sifted as well as Peter. And we can see that the denial of 'Peter' follows on from the failure of 'Simon'. The name Simon is from Simeon, *heard*. Simon is about hearing and heeding, listening and obeying—and it is no coincidence Simon's failure occurs in the Garden of Gethsemane when he cuts off the ear— the organ of hearing—of the high priest's servant.[85]

Old names aren't superseded when God gives us a new name covenant—they're meant to be fulfilled.

Another example of a name redefined occurs in the story of Jabez. Although no obvious name covenant is involved, the story so well illustrates an important principle of naming and re-naming that it is worth examining in some detail. A mere two verses encapsulate the entire life of Jabez:

> *There was a man named Jabez who was more*
> *honourable than any of his brothers. His*

mother named him Jabez because his birth had been so painful. He was the one who prayed to the God of Israel, 'Oh, that You would bless me and expand my territory! Please be with me in all that I do, and keep me from all trouble and pain!' And God granted him his request.

1 Chronicles 4:9–10 NLT

First, let's note where his name comes from: '*His mother named him Jabez because his birth had been so painful.*' Jabez means *pain*. It's also got the name Job within it so it contains that associated meaning as well: *persecution*. In addition, it has an overall sense of why the pain occurred: because of being *walled up*. It seems likely that Jabez was in the breach position during the birth process. He was stuck—for all practical purposes, *walled up*.

Secondly, let's note what Jabez prays. He knows that names encode both destiny and calling and it's clear he doesn't want what his name portends. He doesn't want to give or receive pain, he doesn't want to create or attract trouble and persecution, he doesn't want his life to be walled in, restricted or constrained. So he prayed for the opposite of what his name proclaims as his future: he prayed for the expansion of his inheritance and he prayed that pain would be absent from his life.

And God answered his prayer.

So this means we can pray for God to deal with the negative aspects of our names. All names, by the way, have negative aspects—all names have been claimed by the satan who would like nothing better than to hold our destiny in his hands.

The name 'Jabez' also reveals another principle of renaming. It is essentially the same as 'Jebus', an earlier name for the city of Jerusalem. This name dates from the time when the site was held by the Jebusites. It was David who conquered it from them. The Jebusites had taunted him with a mocking riddle about the blind and the lame taking their fortress. David worked out the riddle but it's clear the defenders were counting on Jebus to live up to its name—for its walls to protect them and for any attackers to retire in pain.

Now, today, Jerusalem is hardly the city of peace its name proclaims—deriving from a combination of 'salem', *peace* and 'yeru', which comes from the root 'yarah', *foundation*.[86] In fact, with the constant bomb threats, terrorist attacks and the Israeli West Bank Wall—the separation barrier along the Green Line border with the Palestinians—it conforms remarkably well to its earlier name: Jebus, *pain*, *persecution* and *walled in*.

The principle we can see in operation here is that renaming does not negate a previous name. But we've already seen that before in the case of Gideon.

It doesn't matter how long ago the renaming was. If a woman takes on her husband's name at marriage, it doesn't sweep her original surname aside so that it has no effect on her calling. If a child receives another name on adoption, that doesn't mean the new entirely supersedes the old. If an author chooses to be known by a pseudonym, the falseness of the name doesn't mean to say it's of no consequence to the writer's identity.

Such thoughts might be alien in the culture of the modern

west, but they are certainly not uncommon in the east. It's not unheard of in some Asian countries to decide that your life is not shaping up the way you'd like and that it needs a little help with a new name—and thus a new destiny. I've ministered to a highly educated Christian who handed me several sheets of parchment, carefully prepared by a village sorcerer at great cost. The new name was specifically designed to ensure health, wealth and happiness in the future. In addition, the sorcerer had worked out the most propitious hour to take on the new name as part of a re-crafted destiny.

The people of the west have almost entirely forgotten how significant names are—but the people of the east remember their intrinsic connection to destiny. Oriental religions, in fact, highlight the relationship between name and breathing. You may recall that God's first recorded word—Hebrew, *be*—is from His own name, *I AM*. From this creative act—the birth of light from God's name—we get a glimpse of how important name covenants are in heaven.

When God breathes a name into us at conception, He gives us a soul. Genesis 2:7 tells us life springs from this name whispered on the breath of God and Psalm 139:15–16 tells us we are 'woven stone'. Our names are woven through our souls.

For this reason, when we are subjected to slander—to mockery, derision and bullying involving our names—it's a blow to the soul. It's a defilement of the holy foundation God placed within us when we were conceived on His breath.

Daniel prophesies about the time when the 'shiqqets shamem'—*the abomination causing desolation*—will be set up on a wing of the Temple. Whatever the literal sense of this—and I believe it is both 'once and future'—I also think it can be applied in a spiritual sense to our own lives. Prophecy is pattern—blueprint which has not only applied historically and given similar circumstances will also apply in the future, but also applies in our individual lives.

And in our individual lives, this phrase 'shiqqets shamem' which hides within itself another phrase, *mockery of the name,* tells us that the deepest desolation comes when we take on ourselves the derision of others about the identity and calling God has given us. When we collude with the enemy and let him occupy a 'wing', we set ourselves up for desolation of soul.

Let us therefore understand religious breathing exercises which involve mantras—encoding the names of godlings—are, in fact, trying to displace the name of God within us and the name He has woven into our souls.

When God offers us a name covenant, He asks us to give Him His breath back. In so doing, we surrender to Him the life, the calling and destiny within our names.

No survey of name covenants between God and mankind would be complete without the most unusual of all—that between Jesus and Mary Magdalene.

In all other instances of a name exchange between God

and a person, it is God who initiates the swap. But in the case of Mary Magdalene, it appears that she is the one who instigates the covenant. Perhaps that's not actually the case but it seems to be that way:

> *Six days before the Passover celebration began, Jesus arrived in Bethany, the home of Lazarus—the man he had raised from the dead. A dinner was prepared in Jesus' honour. Martha served, and Lazarus was among those who ate with him. Then Mary took a twelve-ounce jar of expensive perfume made from essence of nard, and she anointed Jesus' feet with it, wiping his feet with her hair. The house was filled with the fragrance.*

John 12:1–3 NLT

Yep. Here's the signature time period, mentioned yet again: *six days*. The Passover is the archetypal threshold covenant, so those opening words—'*six days before the Passover*'—are a signal to the astute reader that this is going to be a story about a name covenant.

However, the actual exchange is just about as subtle as it's possible to be. And it relies on the reader's knowledge of the testimony in other gospels. Both Mark and Luke narrate this same story, adding other salient details, but neither of them explicitly identifies the woman—although implicitly they certainly do.[87] It is left to John to unambiguously declare who she is, so we can make sense of what transpired in other accounts:

> *And while he was at Bethany in the house of Simon the leper, as he was reclining at table,*

a woman came with an alabaster flask of
ointment of pure nard, very costly, and she
broke the flask and poured it over his head.
There were some who said to themselves
indignantly, 'Why was the ointment wasted
like that?...' And they scolded her. But Jesus
said, 'Leave her alone. Why do you trouble her?
She has done a beautiful thing to Me... She
has anointed My body beforehand for burial.
And truly, I say to you, wherever the gospel is
proclaimed in the whole world, what she has
done will be told in memory of her.'

Mark 14:3–9 ESV

It's not obvious in English. It's not even obvious in Greek. But to a Hebrew reader, it would have been so blatant it was unmissable. John describes the 'fragrance' as *myrrh*. Now Mary's name comes from the same root as myrrh. So the anointing oil she poured over Jesus was her name. And the 'six day' clue tells us something else: she poured it over him the night before His triumphal entry into Jerusalem. Mary was the one who anointed the king just prior to His proclamation by the people.

If there is any doubt this is a name covenant, let it be dispelled by the oil. In Hebrew this is 'shemen' which like 'nashamah', *breath*, and 'neshama', *soul* contains the word 'shem', *name*. We could perhaps even boldly translate 'shemen', *oil*, as *new name, regeneration of name, renewal of name*.

Moreover, if there are any doubts that covenants could be made using oil, Hosea 12:2 and Jeremiah 2:18 dispel that.

This scene, therefore, definitely describes a name covenant. But such a covenant requires an exchange. Mary gave Jesus her name, but what did He give her back? When Simon gave Jesus the name 'Messiah', it's perfectly obvious what Jesus gave him back: Cephas, *cornerstone* or *threshold stone*. Jesus, as the Chief Cornerstone, is perfectly entitled to gift Simon with 'cornerstone'.

This divine name is an allusion to the prophecy of Isaiah:

> *'Therefore thus says the Lord God, "Behold, I am laying in Zion a stone, a tested stone, a costly cornerstone for the foundation, firmly placed. He who believes in it will not be disturbed."'*
>
> Isaiah 28:16 NAS

The word for *cornerstone* here is not 'cephas' but 'pinnah', however the concepts are very much the same—except that 'pinnah' has overtones of a ruby-like gemstone slab while 'cephas' is more ordinary rock with a shallow basin carved into it to collect blood.

Now it shouldn't come as a very big surprise to realise the name Jesus gave to Mary is another allusion to this very same verse in Isaiah. Note that the word 'bachan', *watch-tower*, comes from 'bochan', *tested*, as in *a tested stone*. And Magdalene comes from 'migdol' which also means *watch-tower*, related to *memory*.[88] Jesus is not just saying her story will be remembered; He's telling her she will be the watch-tower, the repository of memory—a prophecy which comes to pass barely a week later when she becomes one of the first witnesses after the Resurrection.

My personal belief is that we can resolve the question of

whether Mary of Bethany is Mary of Magdala very easily. *Yes, they are.* Mary came from Bethany, not Magdala. The confusion comes from the word 'Magdalene'—which I see as the name Jesus gave her when He appointed to be a watchman for the burial she'd just anointed Him for. She was to be a witness to the resurrection and guard the memory of the events surrounding it for all ages to come.

4

Shuttering Heaven

The yiddeoni—the familiar spirits of our family lines—are unbelievably cunning. Take it from me. I've fallen for more than a few of their diabolic tactics over the years, so I feel reasonably qualified to pronounce on their craftiness.

Bear with me: this is the short version of a very complex story.

> I was just putting the finishing touches to a children's fantasy story. It had been, quite literally, that dusty manuscript in a bottom drawer that I'd pulled out and redrafted. At the time I had realised an enormous number of writers were striving—like Jacob wrestling with the angel—with their names. They were not so much plucking a new name from their literary tussles but in various subtle ways redefining an existing one. Perhaps the most obvious was the case of CS Lewis who contended with the Celtic god of light, Llew Llaw Gyffes, *the lion of the steady hand*, and realigned the covenantal imagery with the Lion of Judah. To do this, he created the outstanding literary figure of

Aslan, the Great Lion, who willingly gives his life to save a traitor.

In looking a hundreds of books and finding the same phenomenon repeatedly,[89] I began to wonder what would happen if I took my own writing and deliberately pushed the symbols as far as they would go without breaking them. What would I learn about my own name that I didn't already know? I committed the project to God and eventually I had wordsmithed that old dusty manuscript into a fantasy called *Merlin's Wood—Battle of the Trees* which, just to make things interesting, if not downright confusing, does not feature any appearance by Merlin but does have quite a few symbolic trees— thirteen to be exact.

It felt a fair bit odd to have committed the writing to God and come up with a legend of Merlin and a wood of thirteen different kinds of archetypal trees, all wrapped up in a tale about the nature of forgiveness.[90] I was mulling on this oddity along with the disconcerting fact that I didn't appear to have discovered anything useful about my name—*little did I realise how wrong I was!*—when I got into a conversation with God about names. In the middle of this talk He said something that rocked my world: 'My name is not Yahweh.'

I froze. My warm and friendly chat with God was going disastrously awry. Who exactly was I talking to? Was it possible I was not tuned in to heaven at all, but to someone and something horribly and hellishly different?

'My name,' He continued, 'is Heyah.' At least, that's what it sounded like. It might have been Ehyeh or Hayeh. I was far too flummoxed to ask for the spelling.

It would have been easy to dismiss the conversation as a hijacked moment by a counterfeit spirit—except for one thing. My heart leapt in affirmation: *Yes! Oh yesyesyes! The name of God is truly Heyah.*

It was a terrible and tragic moment. My head of course knew my heart was absolutely and totally deluded. How could I even for a moment consider that God's name throughout Scripture is *not* Yahweh? Or something very similar. The question I knew that occupied many people's minds was the *pronunciation* of Yahweh, not its veracity as the name of God. As I considered my own effusive reaction, I was reminded of Jeremiah's firm conviction: *'The heart is deceitful above all things, and desperately wicked: who can know it?'*[91]

So I immediately shut down all communication with the being who called Himself 'Heyah'. Completely ignorant of name covenants and the fact they generally begin with a self-revelation by God, I was utterly oblivious to any possibility that this was the prelude to a name exchange. And I certainly didn't realise that by shutting out the voice of Heyah, I was refusing to even begin to think about that exchange. I had no idea whatsoever that the name I'd heard is actually found in Scripture and that He was perfectly correct in saying His name is not Yahweh, *He is who He is*. It is indeed Ehyeh, *I Am Who I Am*, as Exodus 3:14 attests. Moreover, it's such a little-known, almost secret name that it has no standard spelling. Heyah, the name I'd heard, is another, but less common, transliteration for it.

I knew none of this. In shuttering the Voice, I was unaware I was closing down my calling, my gifts, my destiny. The door was open and, in a moment of thorough self-sabotage, I slammed it shut myself. Only slowly, ever so slowly, were the gifts and the calling and the destiny re-awakened. At a huge cost. Because, in refusing the call of God, although I didn't realise it, another name covenant seeped in to fill the void. One that I didn't accept— but one that I didn't refuse either. One that I would never have recognised except for the miraculous intervention of God.

Let me reiterate at this point something of critical importance. A name covenant is separate from a blood covenant. Blood covenant is about salvation—and cannot be lost. Once you become a child of God, you can't unbecome His child. A name covenant on the other hand not only has no effect on salvation whatsoever, it is loseable. Once you become a friend of God, you can be unfriended.

So, there I was: I'd refused God's offer of friendship out of sheer ignorance. Worse, I'd shut Him out. Fortunately, just as God never gave up on Moses, He didn't give up on me.

But there was a problem. Not that I had the slightest inkling it existed. The problem was a random story concept that popped into my mind out of nowhere, fully formed. The plot was a mix of science fiction and fantasy and involved a war in another galaxy, a sacred mountain that it was forbidden to climb and a blue nebula that looked like a cow. Although this novel was the absolute lowest tier of priorities among all the books I ever wanted to write in my lifetime—so low that I didn't even set down a single word towards it—the intricacies of its complex plot occupied a fair bit of mental space over half a dozen years. The novel even had a name: *The Ascertainers*. And, I told myself, if I ever wrote it—which I was almost certain would never happen— it would explore the question of how an omnipotent, loving being could allow evil to exist. Many aspects of the book changed over the years as I shifted plotlines around in my head—but the cosmic war, the hallowed mountain and the Blue Cow Nebula were the fixed points around which everything else revolved. It was the strangest of stories: it seemed to lurk in the background of my thoughts but, at the same time, I felt curiously detached from it, even as I spent more and more time developing it.

Fourteen years went by. I discovered that the name God revealed to Moses in Exodus 3:14 was not Yahweh. Even before that, however, my relationship with God had been largely restored and I stepped into the destiny He called me to. He revealed the relationship between the original version of my surname and a wood anciently associated with Merlin. He summoned me across the threshold. And, wonderful God that He is, He didn't tell me what an unholy mess I'd made or what I'd invited into my thoughts until He'd fixed it.

Still I wasted well over a decade, pushing God aside—and although I didn't know it, I needed to deal with a false name covenant that had displaced the one He had wanted for me. As you've probably guessed, it has to do with the story of the forbidden sacred mountain and the Blue Cow Nebula.

I didn't realise the significance of the story until a friend came to visit for several days of prayer ministry. Janice and I intended to specifically pray about the name covenant in her family—and in preparation for the ministry, we prayed for some months that the Holy Spirit would reveal the specific seals surrounding her name. Spiritual seals are identifying symbols which make it possible to discover who holds the title deeds to a person's name. There can be as many as seven seals. They can be booby-trapped—in the sense that, if you try to remove them, you can trigger a curse. Only Jesus can open and remove such seals.

We'd been getting nowhere for three days when Janice began to summarise the spiritual issues in her family line: income, invisibility, integrity, inheritance. *Well*, I thought. *That's the first pattern I've noticed. I wonder if the spirit in question has a name starting with IN.* India was the first word that came to mind.

'No,' the Holy Spirit said. 'But warm.'

Warm? It dawned on me some weeks later I may have been playing a game of *Twenty Questions* with the Holy Spirit. *What's a word like India that's the name of a spirit? Indus? Indonesia?* Somewhere I recalled hearing of a Hindu god named Indra. As I was looking it up on the internet, Janice said: 'I always feel like a pariah.' She paused. 'You know, I'm always saying that, but don't even know what it means.'

And there, flickering in front of me was information about Indra, protector of pariahs—one of the lowest of Hindu castes. Later, once Janice had renounced the covenant in her family line with Indra, I asked the Holy Spirit why He hadn't given us any seals to help us identify this god. 'I threw them at you constantly,' He replied, 'but you didn't recognise any of them.'

That made sense. I knew nothing about Indra prior to looking it up for Janice.

Not long afterwards, she had a strange dream. It recurred three times and had three numbers in it: 5445, 3445, 3443.

Now because my background is mathematics teaching, Janice presented them to me and asked for an interpretation. Well, I multiplied, divided, added, subtracted, factorised, squared, inverted—everything I could think of in all manner of combinations. Finding nothing of significance after a week of playing with the numbers, we scratched around in other places: Strong's numbers, gematria, Scriptural codings.

The breakthrough came just a couple of days later when I had some plumbers in to do some work. The fix was supposed to take half an hour, but took ten. During that time, both the water and the electricity were turned off. Not knowing how long it would take, I decided to do something that could be left at a moment's notice: sort out an old box of papers from my teaching days. During this process, I came across a document on some ancient Hindu mathematics: it described a sequence similar to the Fibonacci numbers which could be used to create a sacred formulation called 'Mount Meru'.

Now, in my small excursion on the internet researching Indra, I had found he was associated with 'Mount Meru'. So I checked to see if the numbers Janice had dreamed of fitted in with this formulation. Incredibly and instantly, I could see the mathematical 'mountain'. And it was obvious that the five 'steps' and the 'footings' of the mountain were not from Indra but from the God of the Christian Scriptures.[92]

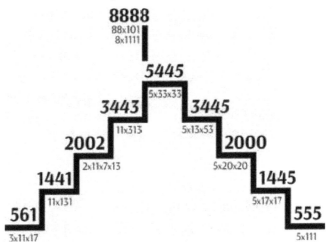

Even if you are not a nerd when it comes to arithmetic, take a minute to appreciate a few hidden treasures of this mathematical 'mountain'. The italicised numbers were given in the dream. They form the summit of a five-step peak with a right-hand footing of 555. This has a factor of 111, the 'number of covenant'. The left-hand footing has a factor of 17, the 'number of Christianity'. 17 is also a factor in the second step of the right-hand side. If the entire formulation is taken beyond the summit, 8888 is obtained. It has factors of 101 and 1111, also a 'number of covenant'. I consider 101 to be the 'number of heavenly provision and sustenance'. In addition 8888 contains the digits 888 which, in gematria, are well-known as referring to Jesus and also Messiah. The left-hand staircase rises in multiples of 11 and the right-hand staircase in multiples of 5.

It was time, in my view, to look a bit more closely at Indra to see what 'Mount Meru' was and what it was counterfeiting. Not long into the investigation, I discovered that Indra had a threshold called an 'indrakila'. The indrakila was sometimes symbolised by a spike or a nail, sometimes by a pillar, sometimes by a doorsill—all of which, in their own way, harked back to Mount Meru, the sacred forbidden mountain of Hindu, Jain and Buddhist cosmology.

Nothing of this was ringing any special bells for me (it was only in retrospect that I realised it should have!) but I decided it was impossible to be too cautious. Especially since I'd spent my life collecting information on mathematical oddities and this was somehow related in to an arithmetical formulation God had brought to Janice's attention. Just on the off-chance there was some defilement flowing down to me, I thought I'd repent of any covenant that might have come down my family line to do with Indra. I'd speak out words of renunciation and revocation and ask Jesus to empower my words.

Having done that, I felt as if I'd wasted my breath: there was no change or even the slightest sense of difference. I almost didn't take the next logical step. But, as I've often said, I'm into overkill when it comes to repentance. Just to be one hundred percent on the safe side, I decided I'd also speak out my repentance of any possible involvement with the indrakila. I hadn't even finished the sentence when *whoosh!* I felt as if a vacuum cleaner had sucked my spirit out.

The shock was as frightening as the sudden spiritual hollowness. *Helphelphelp*, I cried to the Holy Spirit, *I need You now. Nownownownownow*. The void within wasn't filling. *Where are You, Holy Spirit?*

For almost two weeks, I went around feeling drained and empty and calling on the Holy Spirit. Slowly, ever so slowly and gently, the void filled with Him—and when He came, a detachment that I wasn't even aware existed disappeared. I was re-attached to the natural world, to reality—even though I didn't know I'd been disconnected.

I had so many questions I hardly knew where to start. *What is the indrakila and how on earth can it do that?* As I investigated further, this time looking specifically at the connection between Indra and Mount Meru, I discovered he had a herd of blue cows that could be disguised as clouds. And I remembered that science fiction story with the Blue Cow Nebula that had popped into my head about a decade before.

I took it to God. 'What? How? Why?' I asked.

'Remember how I told you My name was "Heyah", not "Yahweh"?' He said. 'I wanted a name exchange.'

It dawned on me that all the work on the novel, praying over it as I pressed into discovering more about my name, was a kind of purification.

'You refused,' God went on. 'Out of ignorance, yes, but that's not relevant. You shut Me out; you closed down the gifts I'd given you. Mount Meru, the indrakila, the beautiful mountain, the threshold of Indra, had just enough of a toehold in your life to be able to come in and fill the void you created.'

'And I came into agreement with the indrakila's presence through the Blue Cow Nebula story I entertained in my head?' I was mortified. A new problem dawned on me. 'I have no idea what to do with the numbers You gave Janice.'

God was silent.

So I made a suggestion. 'I know You have *palmoni*—angels who are number specialists like the one that appears in the Book of Daniel. I'd like to give the numbers to one of them so that they can put these numbers in whatever placement You'd like so they can achieve what You want them to.'

And that's what I did.

And this is how I came to learn that refusing a covenant with God—even when you don't know it's on offer—has dire ramifications.

The yiddeoni are fully aware your ignorance is their opportunity—and they will seize it with all their craft, cunning and might.

The word *wizard* in the King James Version of the Bible translates the word 'yiddeoni'. This is not strictly correct, though there is a relationship: *wizard* derives from *wise* while the yiddeoni are the *knowing ones*—wise from their long and specialised familiarity with particular bloodlines and family trees. The word 'yiddeoni' more accurately means *familiar spirit* and derives from 'yada', *to know*. This is the same word with covenantal overtones we met in relation to Joseph and Pharaoh: '*Now there arose up a new king over Egypt, who knew not Joseph.*' (Exodus 1:8 KJV) For our purposes, better translated: '*Now there arose up a new king over Egypt, who did not have a covenant with Joseph.*'

Yes, we can have covenants with the yiddeoni. In fact, the chances that we have a name covenant with one of these spirits is extremely high. There's a slim chance such a covenant does not include your first name but it will certainly involve your surname. Way back, when one of your ancestors adopted a family name that has been carried on for generations, it's likely the name was dedicated to another god.

If your family name comes from the name of a locality—say, for example, Hamilton, a name I just happen to be particularly familiar with—then you may find that at least one of the familiar spirits of the line is effectively the 'genius loci'. This Latin phrase means *spirit of the place.* The town named Hamilton, near Glasgow in Scotland, is in a locality originally named Cadzow. In fact, some families who originally went by the name 'Cadzow' changed to 'Hamilton'. In the sixth century, this place was on the edge of the Caledonian forest and it was the seat of one of the earliest kings. The stories tell of a Merlin-like figure who roamed the nearby wild wood and a local queen—said to be his sister. Yep, Cadzow was Merlin's wood but that's not what it means. It means, among other things, *battle of the trees.*

When I was writing my young adult fantasy, *Merlin's Wood* with its sub-title, *Battle of the Trees*, I hadn't the slightest inkling of this. In fact, I didn't even have the title until it was finished. I was simply dusting off an older manuscript, looking for the symbols already in it and prayerfully pushing them as far as I could to see if I could discover something about my name. In fact, I was seriously disconcerted when the thirteen trees and their connection to Merlin popped up spontaneously and wouldn't go away.

It was several months before I discovered the connection between my surname and 'Merlin's Wood'. It comes indirectly through the hidden name, Cadzow—the name many Hamiltons were once known by.

This illustrates an important principle—one found repeatedly in Scripture. If you think you can dismiss the spirits of your family line simply by changing your name, forget it.

It doesn't work. The example of Jebus and Jerusalem illustrates that. So too does the change of name of the city of Laish to Dan:

> *They [the men of Dan] went to Laish, to a tranquil and unsuspecting people, and they struck them with their swords and burned down the city. There was no one to deliver them, because the city was far from Sidon and had no alliance with anyone... And the Danites rebuilt the city and lived there. They named it Dan, after their forefather Dan... though the city was formerly named Laish.*
>
> Judges 18:27–29 BSB

Now Laish means *lion*. We're told in Joshua 19:47 Laish was also called Leshem, *treasure* or *treasury*. And Dan means *judge*.

The layering of the name, Dan, with *lion* and *treasure* through this event brings a change into its identity. So great is this change we see that one of the most memorable stories of Daniel, the prophet who proclaimed judgment to both Nebuchadnezzar and his grandson Belshazzar, occurs in a lion's den. Daniel himself is given the name Belteshazzar, *keeper of the secret treasury of Bel*.

The story of the conquering of Laish is entwined in the second-greatest tragedy in Scripture; only the fall in Eden is more disastrous. And the end-result of this calamity—involving the almost complete destruction of the tribal brotherhood through the war on the people of Benjamin—is alluded to in the very next verse about conquering Laish:

> *The Danites set up idols for themselves, and Jonathan son of Gershom, the son of Moses, and his sons were priests for the tribe of Dan until the day of the captivity of the land.*
>
> Judges 18:30 BSB

The great tragedy—Jonathan destroying in a single moment all his grandfather had worked towards for forty years—has its genesis, in my view, in Moses' repeated refusal to accept a name covenant and its associated threshold covenant. I have looked extensively at Jonathan's probable motives in *God's Priority*—and also at how simply Jesus healed this great gash in history on the day of His resurrection. Jesus wasn't taking a casual stroll in the country when He headed for Emmaus—He was binding up the wounds of the past.

You see, it's one thing to be ignorant and turn your back on covenant; it's another entirely to knowingly reject it with deliberate and treasonous calculation.

Moses knew the difference. He knew he was betraying God when he passed over the threshold of the 'lodging' on the road to Egypt. It was Zipporah who re-affirmed covenant with the Lord of the Burning Bush—thus saving her husband's life.

Name covenant is about friendship. You can't betray an enemy. It's when God invites you to a name covenant that the possibility of conscious betrayal, pre-meditated infidelity and intentional, wilful duplicity arises. Of course, these are also possible long before any invitation to a name covenant—however, at the stage of blood covenant, they constitute faithlessless rather than treason.

Name covenant raises the stakes. In a blood covenant with God, He takes on the responsibility for the curses. But in a name covenant, this is no longer the case. Just as Abram was asleep when God made a blood covenant with him, so we too are asleep—dead in our sins—when God blood-covenants with us. But, thereafter, we're awake. He expects us to be alert, watchful and vigilant participants with Him in any further covenants.

Why does it take fourteen years for Abram to become Abraham? Twenty-one years for Jacob to become Israel? A couple of years for Simon to become Cephas—despite the fact Jesus told him what name he'd receive the moment he met Him? It's simple: because true friendship isn't built in a day.

Human beings are intrinsically untrustworthy. Yet God, in His gracious love, allows us to *earn* trust.

Salvation, no. It can never be earned. It must simply be accepted as an undeserved gift. But trust is different. *'God doesn't trust His own servants, and He accuses His angels of making mistakes.'* (Job 4:18 GWT) How much less does He trust humanity? And yet, as we prove ourselves faithful, God risks offering us an extraordinary set of covenants—name, threshold and salt—to bring us into the circle of His friendship.

And we will still fail. Peter did. And Jesus restored him. David did. And God restored him. The elders of Israel who banqueted with God on the sapphire floor did too. But they were not restored.

What's the difference? As Michael Heiser says in *The Unseen Realm*, personal failure is not the same as trading Jesus for another god. And God knows the difference.

Faithfulness is not sinless perfection. It starts with being willing to align our heart with God's purposes for us; it follows up by keeping short accounts through confession and repentance as soon as we become aware of sin; it chooses God over and over and over again in all the decisions of a day; it is appalled to discover its own complicity with His enemy. On being confronted with that complicity and the constriction, wasting and retaliation that is symptomatic of it, it doesn't declare and decree an end to the obstacles and an open door in the heavenlies.

Rather it hastens to say sorry.

If, in the ordinary world, I have a falling-out with a friend and it's my fault, what's going to repair the damage? A sincere and heartfelt apology? Or a passionate public declaration that nothing's going to tear us apart?

If we can't bring ourselves to apologise—if we've inculcated that legal mindset that says 'never admit liability' but which effectively amounts to 'never say sorry'—then we're prepared to sacrifice the relationship on the altar of self-interest.

God calls us to truth. To love. To mercy. To justice. To peace.

Not to self-preservation.

Because that allows the yiddeoni to continue to quietly and unobtrusively continue directing our thoughts and guiding our actions.

When our ancestors have traded away a name—often on migrating to another country and finding their foreign-sounding name was a social disadvantage—it may not have been an exchange with another human being. But, in the spiritual, it can be an exchange with a godling. As I have worked with people, helping them understand the covenants over their names, sometimes they'll tell me that God is talking to them about a new name. And it turns out it's not new at all—it's old. It comes from one or two generations back when dad or granddad decided to disguise his heritage in order to fit in better in a new community.

So many of us have unfinished business with the past. Just as Jerusalem has unfinished business with Jebus.

How do we deal with the ungodly name covenants affecting our bloodlines? Or marriage? I look at the struggles of hundreds of authors and see the same sort of wrestle with the angel that Jacob experienced. But for many others I see nothing at all. Why do some people spend their lives in a fight to the death with the yiddeoni and others remain untroubled by them?

I believe it all depends on our attitude towards the threshold. As soon as we commit ourselves to coming into the unique destiny God has for us—to devote our efforts towards achieving the singular purpose for which He created us—we become targets.

If you just want to make money, have a comfortable life or enjoy what the world has to offer, you're no danger to the powers of hell. If you just want fame and the trappings of glamour and success, you still constitute no threat to the enemies of God. Even if you want to indulge in thrills or sensory exhilaration of various kinds—most of them morally neutral—you're not going to trouble the prince of this world.

But as soon as you decide, even somewhat selfishly, that nothing's going to stop you heading down the path God planned for you when He breathed your name into you and gave you a soul, then the yiddeoni go to yellow alert. Deciding to be faithful to your calling is not the same as being faithful to God but it might lead to it. And that's a full red alert situation. As you approach the threshold and the possibility of an invitation from God to 'pass over' becomes more likely, ungodly threshold guardians make their appearance. The first you're likely to encounter is the spirit of forgetting—the spirit of tearing truth apart. If this spirit can derail you by attacking your memory, then you may not even meet any other threshold sentinels.

But if you keep going then perhaps you'll wrestle with the angel like CS Lewis did. In his works, he tussles with the Celtic god of light, Llew *the lion*, in order to rededicate his name to the Light of the World and Lion of Judah. In addition, in his epic poem *Dymer*, published before he became a Christian, he began his long grapple with some famous characters of Arthurian legend: Morgan and Merlin. I recognise these as familiar spirits of the Hamilton line and I find it to be no coincidence Lewis was using the name Clive Hamilton as a pseudonym when he wrote these poems.

One of the most remarkable examples of names affecting an individual's writing output is the case of Nobel Prize winner, Toni Morrison. As I've pointed out in *God's Priority*, the imagery of her stories as well as the specific names within them match her surname, Morrison, with uncanny accuracy. That isn't a surprise. What is quite stunning is this: Morrison isn't the name she was born with—it's her ex-husband's surname. Even more astonishing is this: she is Afro-American while the names and allied symbolism she uses is uniquely associated with the Morrisons of the Outer Hebrides in Scotland.[93] A thin veneer of Afro-American imagery hides a deep bedrock of Celtic myth—demonstrating that, at least in her case, racial background is less significant than the name she adopted!

There are hundreds of other authors, far less well-known

than these, whose writings show they are engaged in a tensely fought struggle with the daemons—the yiddeoni—who have a covenant with the family. On a conscious level, we may not even be aware of the existence of the yiddeoni. But, when we start to write and to reveal the deep desires of our hearts, we find that what comes up time and again is a desperate longing to be free of these rapacious beings. Christian or not, the stories of many authors show how deeply they yearn to fling off the yoke of the yiddeoni and come into covenant with the One who calls Himself, 'I AM'.

In retrospect, it's no coincidence that—as I prayed over a book in which I hoped to discover more about my own name—God was in the process. I didn't start out with a plot idea about thirteen trees but that flowed naturally in as I noticed a different kind of tree in the first four chapters and decided to keep the motif going. Nor did I start out with any plans to talk about Merlin: that segued in because I wanted to introduce the concept of tachyons—elemental particles from theoretical physics that, if they exist, travel backwards in time. It's a short step from particles that travel backwards in time to TH White's depiction of Merlin in the *Once and Future King* as living backwards in time. As one draft moved to another and I wrestled with the words, I didn't realise I was really wrestling with God about my own name. No wonder as I drew towards the end of the final draft, He introduced Himself with a new name.

No wonder CS Lewis found the 'Lion bounding in' as he set out to write about the picture of the faun and the lamp-post that had been recurring in his mind's eye for decades.

Perhaps you're thinking: 'But I don't write fantasy! I don't write fiction! What do I do instead? How am I going to wrestle like Jacob? How is God going to talk to me?'

The fact is: even in Scripture, not everyone wrestled like Jacob. Moses was offered covenant simply for making the decision to 'turn aside' and look at a mysterious bush that was burning but not turning to ash. Gideon was hiding in a wine press, Simon was answering a question, Solomon wasn't capable of doing much other than bawl—he was just a baby when God told the prophet Nathan to tell King David that His name for Solomon was Jedidiah. David means *beloved* and Jedidiah is *beloved of God*—it is in fact a play on David's own name. It's interesting that this name wasn't used. Was this another case of refusing name covenant? Certainly God becomes angry with Solomon late in his life because He'd appeared to him twice but Solomon still turned away.[94]

Jedidiah is prophetic, nonetheless, just as Immanuel is: it points to a later Son of David, the *beloved* Son who dwells with us.

Still what can ordinary people today do to tackle their name issues? No one's ordinary—ordinary is just the stage of extraordinary-in-waiting we all go through prior to passing over into our calling.

Leitangi's dad died just before she was born. It was such a shock to her mum that she went into labour and gave birth to a premature baby girl. Leitangi's grandparents were elders in Vanuatu who helped the local missionaries. They came to the thatched hut with its dirt floor kitchen and wrapped Leitangi's hands and feet in cotton wool, because she had no nails. When the mission boat came in, the missionaries went to the ship and bought cans of condensed milk to feed Leitangi. Surrounded by love—including that of a heavenly Father—she grew to be strong and healthy. Her name was chosen to remember her earthly father: Leitangi means *lady of mourning* or *lady of sorrows*.

Leitangi didn't like her name. Imagine, she says, people calling out to you, 'Hey, Lady of Sorrow!'

Leitangi grew up during colonial times in the New Hebrides. The languages spoken there were French and English. On her first day at a French kindergarten, Leitangi was introduced by the Vietnamese maid to the teacher as 'Martine'. Apparently her given name was considered unpronounceable!

Just a year or so later, Leitangi began Grade 1 at an Anglican school. The teacher there said to her that from then on, her name would be 'Martina' because 'you are now in an *English* school.'

And that is how she has been known even to today. When Martina went to boarding school, a guest preacher came in one day. It was the missionary and his wife who had saved her life! She wanted to go up and introduce herself but she was too shy. However two weeks later, when she went home for the holidays, she came back from shopping to see a woman talking to her mother. 'How is your daughter?' the woman asked in her mother's language. Her mother pointed to her and said, 'Leitangi.'

The woman grabbed her hands and looked at her fingernails and toenails. 'Perfect!' she said.

In 1986, Martina was 'born again'. A sister pastor laid hands on her and, praying, saw in a vision a handwoven basket coming down from heaven. Inside the basket was the strip of paper with the name 'Mary'. 'Today,' she said, 'God has given you a new name: Mary.'

'That sits well with me,' Martina says.

No wonder! For in some traditions, Mary, the mother of Jesus, was often called *the lady of sorrows* because of the prophecy of Simeon at the circumcision of Jesus. '*A sword will pierce your very soul.*' (Luke 2:35 NLT)

And, just as Leitangi was named for *remembrance*, so too Mary is associated with remembrance through its association with Magdalene, Jesus' chosen guardian of memory.[95] The names, Leitangi and Mary, are very, very different. But the same resonances are there. The song of the two names harmonises beautifully.

This is a general, but by no means universal, rule. When God gives us a new name, it will be associated in a poetic, symphonic way with some aspect of the name we already have or with part of our family heritage.

When Josie told me the new name God had given her I was baffled. I couldn't see any relationship between that name and her own. But then she revealed one of her ancestors, on migrating to a new country, had wanted to fit in and succeed in business. So he had dropped his surname and adopted that of a local dignitary. The name God had given her was the original surname before the change! Now that made sense! Of course God was returning the very thing that should never have been forfeited in the first place.

Janine's story attests to this:

> Late in 2016, I received a word from a good friend: 'Janine, God has a word for you—but this is for Janine, not Violeti.' I had changed my name from Janine to Violeti ten years previously out of rebellion and rejection towards my father. It was also intended to be a way for me to receive favour and an inheritance.

> A little over a month after I received this word I traveled to Aitutaki in the Cook Islands, my homeland. My father travelled with me. He had been adopted out at the age of seven because his mother died; he had not been back to Aitutaki for forty years! At the time of his mother's death, he'd been parcelled out along with his ten siblings to various relatives. As a result, he'd been abused all his teenage life.

> It so happened that, while we were in Aitutaki, the carer who abused him also returned at the same time. Many decades had passed and she was now aged and very weak. She was nice to my dad. However the anger my father had towards her was very obvious. Yet the most unlikely thing had happened. This woman, along with her daughter, my father's brother and other family members all gathered together to help my father get his inheritance back.

By the end of our trip my father had his land given to him in a matter of just three days! God was with all over that! Redeemed inheritance and restored relationships!

While I was in the plane flying back to Australia, the Lord showed me a vision. The vision is of a section of land with *my* name on it. I thought God was showing that since, because my dad has his inheritance back, that means that as a descendant I am entitled to that piece. Then the Holy Spirit shows me again: 'Janine, look at the map again.'

He called me 'Janine', not Violeti—and then I see my name written on the map as Janine not Violeti. I made a decision in my heart: *I need to change my name back.*

Through a series of miracles, I met for coffee with Anne Hamilton who backed up so much for me and gave me the final confirmation that pushed me to take action. The next week I was signing forms and getting things in place so I can change my name.

A little while later, I was finalising more things for my name change. As I was going to sleep one night, the Lord placed the name 'Jacob' on my heart. So I decided to go and pray for Jacob in my lounge. I started to intercede for Jacob, even though I had no idea who Jacob was or what I was supposed to be praying for. The next day I went to work and I asked everyone if they had a relative by the name of Jacob who needed prayer. No one responded. No one even had an idea who this Jacob could be. Another night went by and the Lord brought Jacob to my mind again. I began to pray once more. The next day I decided to go and do some reading on Jacob and Esau and research some teachings by my favourite prophetic teachers to see if there was something I was missing. Funnily enough, I didn't find anything!

But that night I heard the Lord whisper, 'Janine, are you ready to know who Jacob is?'

I cried out, 'Yes, oh goodness yes! Who is he?'

The Holy Spirit whispered, 'You are Jacob.'

I'm like: 'Huh?'

The Holy Spirit then started to go through the story of Esau and Jacob. He said to me, 'When I asked Jacob, "What is your name?" I didn't ask him because I didn't know his name, I was asking him to confess who he was. He tried to fool his dad, but I was letting him know he cannot fool Me. Therefore when he said to Me, 'It's me, Jacob,' he stopped the games and surrendered who he was. It was then I released his new name to him: *Israel*.'

I started to weep and repented non-stop. I was a mess! I realised what I'd done for the last eleven years! I'd been walking around with the name 'Violeti', trying to get favour, trying to earn favour, out of an orphan heart. Yet all the time God had named me Janine, *favour of God*!

I wept because of His mercy and the grace to be able to change my name back and still receive everything He'd promised. Next day, Papa started to minister to me about how Jacob reacted out of the rejection of his father as well. It was a beautiful lesson to go through. I am happy to say I now embrace my name 'Janine'.

God is still in the business of covenanting with us about names. Whether it's restoring a lost name, tweaking a name by the addition of a letter or two, redefining the meaning of a name, bestowing on us the name we should always have received at birth—whatever way He chooses to craft the lyric of the calling within our names—He is establishing His covenant masterwork in us.

All names come from Him. Yet this is not at all the same as saying that every name belongs to Him.

Yes, all names come from the Father. Paul acknowledges this when he says that God is the ultimate source of all names: '*I kneel before the Father, from whom every family in heaven and on earth derives its name.*' (Ephesians 3:14–15 NIV)

Yet, as I said, this does not mean that every name

currently belongs to Him. God bestowed on humanity the privilege of naming when He gave His regent, Adam, a remarkable honour:

> Now the Lord God had formed out of the ground all the wild animals and all the birds in the sky. He brought them to the man to see what he would name them; and whatever the man called each living creature, that was its name. So the man gave names to all the livestock, the birds in the sky and all the wild animals.
>
> Genesis 2:19–20 NIV

This gift—the gift of naming, thus of prophetically proclaiming the identity and destiny of all living things—was the first God gave to Adam, after that of life itself. The satan desires to possess names above all else and, if he can't rob us of them, he wants to destroy them—possibly because he doesn't have a name of his own.[96] Unfortunately when Adam disobeyed God and effectively handed over his regency of the earth to the satan this was part of the package.

The satan is routinely called the 'father of lies' throughout Scripture but, whether in Greek or Hebrew, the various words for *lies* are always rooted in a word for *slander*. And slander is about corrupting reputations and wrecking names. This is reinforced by the revelation in Ezekiel 28 that the satan was cast out of heaven because of sin that came through violence resulting from trade—this word, *trade*, is derived from a word that can also mean *gossip, slander, calumny, informant, scandal-monger*. The implication is that the satan trades in names. This might seem strange at first. But why should it? Think about it:

the satan counterfeits all that God does, and a name trade is simply an imitation of a divine name covenant.

It's because of the existence of these counterfeits that it's so important to listen closely and carefully to God when He begins to talk to us about names. Because name covenants are not just about friendship with Him, they are about overcoming the satan.

Jesus asks John to write to the angel of the church of Pergamum, where the throne of the satan is: '*To the one who is victorious, I will give some of the hidden manna. I will also give that person a white stone with a new name written on it, known only to the one who receives it.*' (Revelation 2:17 NIV)

To the people of the first century, a white stone was about victory. Champions at the Olympic Games received a white stone with their name on it, as well as a laurel wreath or a wild olive crown. In a courtroom, a guilty verdict was signified by a black stone and innocence by a white one. Entry tokens for festivals were sometimes white stones. So white stones of John's era symbolised attainment, acquittal and admittance.

But the white stone God promises the ones who stand and overcome has a secret name on it. The aspect of secrecy is significant—after all, what distinguishes a friend from an acquaintance is the sharing of secrets.

This is what we see happen just a few days after Abram becomes Abraham, God drops by to visit and adds a threshold covenant and a salt covenant to the name covenant—the exchange of El Shaddai and Abraham. God debates with

Himself as to whether He will conceal His purpose in heading towards Sodom and Gomorrah, deciding to reveal that He has come to judge the cities of the plain.

As the result of the name exchange that happens during this period, Abram not only becomes Abraham, *covenant father of nations*, but a friend of God. And when Sarah gives birth to Isaac in the fullness of time, Abraham's destiny as that ancestor of nations is secured. So it might seem bizarre that, a decade or so later, that God asked Abraham to sacrifice the very same destiny he'd been given through that new name. God asked Abraham to offer up his son, Isaac.

Now, of course, there were many, many nuances going on when God made that request. Here's another of them: when God gives us a name covenant and brings us over the threshold into our calling, we step into our destiny—and the temptation is to place our identity in that destiny *instead of in God*.

And that why sometimes—just sometimes—God seems to turn around and demand of us the very destiny He's just gifted to us. Because we're in danger of placing our identity in the gift and not in the Giver.

After his name covenant, after the name exchange when Abram became Abraham and fathered Isaac, his identity was in danger of becoming fused with his destiny as the *father of nations*. Identity has always to be in God, not in our destiny. This is why, sometimes, God will ask us to sacrifice our destiny.

Because a gift in which your identity lies is an exceptionally dangerous gift.

By now, I hope you have some appreciation for the enormity of the gift God is offering when He begins talking to you about name covenant. However, just because He tells you He's got a new name for you doesn't mean that it's ready for you to adopt immediately. Simon was told by Jesus at their first meeting that he would be called 'Cephas'. However it was almost exactly two years by the Hebrew calendar—except, so it appears, for two days—before that particular name exchange actually eventuated, just as Jesus prophesied. Still, the foreshadowing of that covenant was well and truly apparent the very moment they met.

The circumstances of their encounter began with Andrew, Simon's brother, who whenever he's mentioned in the gospels, is always leading people to Jesus. Perhaps this is why, when the satan gets his hooks into the name Andrew, it always seems to be that it's about undoing the good that people with that name have done for the Kingdom. There is a spirit which specialises in following after people to defile and destroy the good they've achieved, so that whatever they've managed to build up falls down after they've left. Goodness and mercy should follow us, not defilement and destruction.

Now the apostle Andrew had been on the scene to hear John the Baptist say: 'Look, there is the Lamb of God!' And so, with another disciple, he followed Jesus. Then he went off to find Simon, and brought him around to introduce him to Jesus. The next day a group of them, by this time including Nathanael and Philip, headed off for Galilee. From the clues scattered through the text, there is a six-day period between the time John the Baptist is quizzed by the scribes and Pharisees and denies that he is the Messiah until the apostles all arrive in Galilee and the events of the wedding feast in Cana unfold.

Now six days is of course the signature time span between a name and a threshold covenant. Is there a threshold covenant taking place at Cana? Well, certainly there is a threshold and it involves Jesus—He performs His first miracle by changing water into wine and, as a consequence, His public ministry begins. In fact, the very name 'Cana' testifies to the threshold nature of what transpired. Cana means *reeds*. Now perhaps the word *reeds* doesn't automatically evoke *threshold* in your mind. But consider: reeds grow in the transition zone between land and water. They occupy shorelines and riverbanks. They mark the edge, just as a threshold denotes the boundary between inside and outside at a doorway or gate.

In fact, one of the words for *reeds*, 'suph', is actually related to 'saph', *threshold*.[97] And because reeds mark a transition zone just as a threshold does, it makes me wonder if the 'Yam Suph' which the Israelites crossed during their exodus from Egypt was ever meant to be translated as either the *sea of reeds* or the Red Sea. Perhaps it would be better rendered as *waters of transition* or *the threshold sea*.

Such controversial possibilities aside, let's return to John, baptising in the Jordan. Since the wedding at Cana seems to begin on the feast of Sukkot, then by back-dating six days, it appears John denied that he was the Messiah on the Day of Atonement, Yom Kippur. The next day he points out Jesus as the 'Lamb of God'. Is a divine name covenant occurring here? Perhaps. It's hard to tell. But if it is, then what name does John receive in the exchange? Could it be '*the voice of one crying in the wilderness*'? Certainly, another John many years later was told to seal up the words of the 'voice of seven thunders'. To 'seal' is to use a stamp of identity and in that phrase, *voice of seven thunders*, there is a unity of two identities—the voice and the thunder, the first claimed by John the Baptist and the second given by Jesus to the apostle John as one of the 'sons of thunder'.

It does not seem a coincidence that this is a foreshadowing of the name covenant between Simon and Jesus, almost precisely two years later, when Simon gave Jesus the title 'Messiah' and Jesus dubbed him 'Cephas', the cornerstone or threshold stone. Nor does it seem coincidence that the glory of Jesus is revealed in the first situation through His first public miracle. In the second instance an even higher level of glory is evident during His transfiguration on the top of a mountain.

It is as Paul says: '*So all of us, with faces unveiled, see as in a mirror the glory of the Lord; and we are being changed into His very image, from one degree of glory to the next, by Adonai the Spirit.*' (2 Corinthians 3:18 CJB)

Glory to glory to glory. That is His promise. Yet, as we can see, it is not for us to determine the timing of these covenants. God may let us know well in advance what He has planned for us, as He did for Simon Peter. Or He may not. Both the timing and the invitation is entirely the prerogative of the Lord of Time who is also—mightily and wondrously—the redeemer of our wasted time.

5

Naming His Names

How many names does God have? El Shaddai, *almighty nurturer*; Yahweh, *ever-existing one*; Yahweh-Jireh, *provider*; Yahweh-Nissi, *banner*; Yahweh-Saboath, *army commander*; Adonai, *lord*; Yahweh-Maccaddeshem, *sanctifier*; Yahweh-Rohi, *shepherd*; Yahweh-Shammah, *present one*; Yahweh-Rapha, *healer*; Yahweh-Tsidkenu, *righteous one*; Yahweh-Ghmolah, *giver of recompense*; El-Elyon, *most high God*; El-Gibbor, *mighty warrior*; El-Olam, *everlasting one*; El-Roi, *one who sees*; El-Shaddai-Rohi, *mighty shepherd of Jacob*; El-Chuwl, *creator who gives us birth*; El-Deah, *god of wisdom and knowledge*; Attiyq Youm, *Ancient of Days*.

Yet all of these titles barely scratch the surface of the surface. The number of His names must surely be uncountable. After all, every name in heaven and on earth comes from Him. And since, as Psalm 147:4 NLT says, '*He counts the stars and calls them all by name*,' this means a billion trillion or so. Just for starters. Just the ones we can see in the visible universe!

There are also many hidden stars and they too must have names. In many ways, these hidden ones are like the names of God veiled in Scripture. We've already seen one: '*My name is war*' hidden as a layer of '*My name is in him*'.

And another: '*Watchtower*' edged with '*Remembrance*' from the exchange Jesus made with Mary Magdalene, and which is poetically related to *tested*, describing the Chief Cornerstone set in Zion.

Could we even count 'hidden' itself as one of the names of God? The Persian name Esther means *star*. More specifically, *morning star*. It's a reference to Ishtar, a goddess of love and war. However, it sounds just like the Hebrew word, 'astir', which denotes *hiddenness* or *concealment*. The Book of Esther is the only book of Scripture in which the name of God does not appear. But then it is the book of hiddenness, concealment and masked identities. Esther's original name was Hadassah, *myrtle*. When the myrtle flowers, its blossoms are a froth of tiny white stars, reminding us of the meaning of Esther.

Perhaps the most famous line in this orphan-is-chosen-as-queen story is found in the words of her guardian Mordecai. He challenges her to her to go to the king and risk her life to save her people:

> '*For if you remain silent at this time, relief and deliverance will arise for the Jews from another place and you and your father's house will perish. And who knows whether you have not attained royalty for such a time as this?*'
>
> Esther 4:14 NIV

For such a time as this.

With these words, he's speaking directly into both her identity and destiny. For him, she's still 'Hadassah', *myrtle*, from a root word meaning *the appointed time*.

Esther of course eventually saves her people. Her story is prophetic of the hidden, unrecognised Saviour. He is not only hidden, 'astir', He claims the title of the morning star and thus the name of Esther—'*I, Jesus, have sent My angel to testify to you these things in the churches. I am the root and the offspring of David, and the bright and morning star.*' (Revelation 22:16 KJV) Esther's name is a direct reference to the morning star. Which is, of course, the planet Venus. And Venus is also the evening star.[98]

Now from time to time, the planet Venus passes between the earth and the sun and disappears from the sky. This is the time of its transition from being the 'evening star' to becoming the 'morning star'. Generally it's hidden from sight for three days.

This ancient queen of Persia was not just Hadassah of *the appointed time*, the one destined for a time such as this, she was also Esther, *the hidden* in one language and *the star* in another. Her three-day fast (mentioned in Esther 4:16) may well reflect this double aspect of her name.

At the end of Esther's three-day fast, she went to the king to plead for her people. Her action is prophetic of the ascent of Jesus, *the bright and morning star*, to the Father after His three days, *hidden* in the tomb.

Some people get hung up on the possibility that the word 'Easter' may come from Esther or Ishtar, via an incredibly obscure Anglo-Saxon goddess, Ēostre. Nothing is known about Ēostre except a single brief mention by the eighth century historian who says that, in the past, feasts were held in her honour. Attempts to connect her with eggs and hares are pure speculation. And if speculation is allowed,

I suggest that 'Easter' could well have another meaning: *the star that passes over* or *the angel that passes over*.[99]

Once we start to say that certain names are 'pagan'—that 'Easter' derives from Ishtar, for example[100] —we not only deny that every family in heaven and on earth derives its name from the Father, we also deny all that Jesus did to redeem these names.

Through many centuries, the prophets of Israel and Judah denounced both Ishtar in her local guise, Asherah, as well as her consort, Tammuz. One of the principal titles of this Chaldean god was the *Bread Come Down From Heaven* and one of Asherah's titles as a protector of sailors was *She Who Walks On Water*.

It is no coincidence that Jesus walked on water on the very same day as He performed the miracle of the loaves and fishes and announced that He was the *Bread of Life* and the *Bread Come Down From Heaven*. He took on both Asherah and Tammuz on the same day. He claimed back from them the very titles that they had usurped and which belonged to His Father.

To say that Easter is a pagan word denies this work of Jesus on our behalf. While the satan has engaged in identity theft, trading in names and destinies, souls and lives, Jesus has restored all that was stolen. He was continually in conflict over names. John's gospel records how He took back from the enemy seven divine names that had been stolen: *The Light of the World*, *The True Vine*, *The Good Shepherd*, *The Gate of the Sheep*, *The Way, The Truth and the Life*, *The Resurrection and The Life*, as well as *The Bread Come Down From Heaven*.

Symbolically, seven represents completeness, so Jesus retrieved *all* of God's titles that had been usurped by the gods of the nations. Yet many Christians concede the claims of the Enemy in this regard and do not understand Jesus has made it possible for the restoration of all names to their rightful owners. Every time we agree Christmas has its roots in a pagan solstice festival or that Easter is the name of an Anglo-Saxon goddess, we deny the full accomplishment of Jesus on the cross.

The seven names Jesus especially targeted were:

I AM the bread of life.

- John 6:35— I am the bread of life. He who comes to Me will never go hungry, and he who believes in Me will never be thirsty.
- John 6:48— I am the bread of life
- John 6:51— I am the living bread that came down from heaven.

I AM the light of the world.

- John 8:12— I am the light of the world. Whoever follows Me will never walk in darkness, but will have the light of life.
- John 9:5— While I am in the world, I am the light of the world.

I AM the door.

- John 10:7— I tell you the truth, I am the gate for the sheep.

I AM the good shepherd.

- John 10:11— I am the good shepherd. The good shepherd lays down His life for the sheep.

I AM the resurrection and the life.

- John 11:25— I am the resurrection and the life. He who believes in Me will live, even though he dies.

I AM the way, the truth and the life.

- John 14:6— I am the way and the truth and the life. No one comes to the Father except through Me.

I AM the true vine.

- John 15:1, 5— I am the true vine, and My Father is the gardener. I am the vine; you are the branches. If a man remains in Me and I in him, he will bear much fruit; apart from Me you can do nothing.

In each of these sayings, Jesus consistently used the phrase 'I am...'—equating Himself with God, the great I AM. Was it for this reason He lost most of His followers when He came out with the first of these statements, 'I AM the bread of life'? He'd just performed a mind-bending miracle: multiplying five barley loaves and two fish, distributing them to over five thousand people and still having masses of fragments left over. Let's not overlook those fish: is there a Hebrew word describing both grain and fish? Again, we have to look to the poetry: 'dagan' is *grain* and 'dagah' is both *fish* and *multiplication*.

The farmers and fishermen witnessing the miracle would have understood the principle. Jesus did exactly what

God does quietly and routinely as one season rolls into the next. God created fish to breed, causing their stocks increase dramatically. He created a head of barley to grow from a single seed sown in the soil: to multiply its yield.

Jesus telescoped the time between 'sowing' and 'harvest' together, showing He is Lord of Time as well as Lord of the Harvest. In addition, besides taking on Tammuz, He also broke in pieces the Philistine god Dagon, whose name is so similar to 'dagan', *grain*, and 'dagah', *fish*.

While we're looking at these particular ramifications of what Jesus did, let's ask a difficult question: what makes this event a miracle and not magic? Let's consider the temptation of Jesus in the wilderness to answer that. In essence, what the satan asked Jesus to do during the first temptation was magic: to change stones into bread. Jesus, as He Himself testifies, only does what He sees the Father doing—and the Father always creates things *after their own kind*. Not stones from bread, but bread from bread. There's no question in my mind that Jesus could have turned stones into bread but He chose not to. That would have been using God's creative principles against the will of God. And that's the simplest definition of magic: activating the power God has put into words, symbolism and ceremony to use it against Him.

Returning to examine the events of the day Jesus pushed back at Asherah, Tammuz and Dagon, we have to wonder why the people turned against Him. He was simply reclaiming for the Father all that had been stolen for so long. What upset the people so much when they'd just experienced God's grace in a wondrous and tangible way? They were, after all, expecting and hoping for the Messiah. They wanted God to visit His people. Even if they weren't quite prepared to credit that Jesus was God-come-in-the-flesh, they might have considered Him to be an angelic messenger.

And even if there were reasons to discount that possibility, human beings are still apt to put up with a fair degree of eccentricity—even heresy—when free food is on the table. Jesus Himself said as much: He accused the people of following Him simply because He gave them bread. So why didn't they give Him the benefit of the doubt? Why did they mutter, 'This is a hard saying' and feel they had to leave?

It's my view the problem was not so much the 'I am' at the beginning of each of these statements, but what comes after. Taken as a totality, every one of these sayings is an iconoclastic shattering of the prevailing Hebrew worldview.

Remember that the Jews were a people chafing under Roman rule. By law, a soldier could command any man to carry a load for a mile. The Jews were familiar with the customs of their conquerors. Men like the centurion who impressed Jesus with his declaration of faith lived side by side with the locals. So the Jews would have immediately recognised the words, 'the light of the world'. Jesus didn't make it up on the spot. It might have belonged to His Father but, as far as the Jews were concerned, it was a title of the Persian god, Mithras, a particular favourite of Roman soldiers.

Jesus was blatantly provocative when He said: 'I am the Light of the World.' To His audience, it would have seemed a blasphemous mix of God's name with that of Mithras.

The title 'Bread of Life' was no less shocking. Perhaps it was even worse because Ezekiel had explicitly warned the people against mixing worship of Yahweh with worship of Tammuz: *'...he brought me to the entrance to the north gate of the house of the Lord, and I saw women sitting there, mourning for Tammuz.'* (Ezekiel 8:14 NIV) The practice of syncretism—the mixing of pagan rites with worship of the true God— had brought disaster on Israel six centuries previously. And many times since.

Pious Jews were ready to welcome the Messiah—the one they believed would proclaim liberty and freedom for the captives, even if they interpreted this as expelling the Roman overlords—but the price Jesus seemed to be asking was way too high. The people had been warned time and time again about hedging their bets by worshipping other gods. Yet the 'hard saying' of Jesus was His apparent claim that He, Yahweh and Tammuz were one. No wonder so many people left without a backward glance. They didn't comprehend that He was taking back the name; they didn't see the victory over the old gods; they saw complicity and accommodation with demonic ruling powers.

Jesus, in fact, was far from finished with His hard sayings. 'The true vine' was a title of the Cretan god Dionysus-Zagreus, the wild wine-loving deity who revelled in orgy, destructive mutilation and ritual madness. Worship of the Roman version of Dionysus—Bacchus—became so extreme and violent, involving random murder, rape and other atrocities, that it was actually banned!

'I am the gate' or 'I am the door' was a reference to Janus, the oldest of the Roman gods, the double-faced keeper of doorways and gates after whom the month of January is named. He is a godling of first and last things, of openings and closings, beginnings and endings—so perhaps Luke was evoking this when he began his narrative of Jesus' birth by noting its historical setting: *'...the first census that took place while Quirinius was governor of Syria.'* (Luke 2:2 NIV)

Quirinius, *powerful man of peace*, was a title of Janus. Originally a rustic pastoral deity, Janus had many rituals concerned with war and peace.[101] One of the ancient laws connected with him was *spolia opima*: a ceremony involving the stripping of a defeated enemy king slain in single combat. It included an offering to Janus Quirinus and the sacrifice of a lamb. The stripping of Jesus, the Lamb of God and the Door of the Sheep, strongly echoes this rite. And the reversal, the overturning of the power of Janus, is found in Paul's words: *'But thanks be to God, who always leads us as captives in Christ's triumphal procession and uses us to spread the aroma of the knowledge of him everywhere.'* (2 Corinthians 2:14 NIV)

Jesus also claimed 'The Good Shepherd', a title of Pan, a Greek god of flock and herds as well as the countryside. Pan inspired sudden fear: thus the word 'panic'.

Those listening to Jesus would have detected allusions to well-known divinities of Rome, Crete, Persia, Chaldea and Greece. It is likely that the gods in question were the most ancient ones of each nation mentioned. The 'resurrection and the life' may have been a title of Osiris, one of the chief gods of Egypt.[102]

Jesus had set His sights on reclaiming *names* for the Kingdom of God. He was not defying the Shema—*Hear O Israel, the Lord is our God, the Lord is One*[103] —and suggesting Yahweh was actually a sevenfold gang of gods, most of whom enjoyed dark and dubious reputations. He was pointing out the major titles of God that had been usurped and using signs to show He had the privilege of restoring them to the Father. He was engaging in war with the various dark spiritual princes who held sway over various territories and who have claimed these titles as their own.

He took that war over names right onto the turf these angelic majesties[104] had most emphatically claimed for themselves. In doing so, He set His church a task—to bring back names to their true owner: the Father. There are far more than seven names Jesus wants back. He wants them all. And He declared His intention to redeem them in the most spectacular way: with a combined name and threshold covenant. This covenant was for His church, His ekklesia—and it's a parallel to the one at Mount Sinai where God declared, 'My name is war.'

This name covenant, on the surface, appears to be one with Simon. But it goes deeper: it's not, in fact, with Simon as an individual, it's with him as the founding member of the ekklesia. You see, Simon was far from the first person to say that Jesus was the Messiah. Andrew said it (John 1:41), based simply on the testimony of John the Baptist. The Samaritans of Shechem, influenced by the testimony of the woman Jesus spoke to at Jacob's Well, said so too (John 4:29; 42). Some of the people of Jerusalem agreed He was the Messiah (John 7:41). Now, while the timings of the last two incidents are unclear, Andrew's words occur even before Jesus starts His public ministry—before He has performed a single miracle.

So when Simon confesses Jesus as the Messiah, He's only confirming what Andrew told him two years previously. But now the moment has finally come and Jesus is ready—ready to declare war to take back what the satan had plundered through his trade in names: identities, destinies, lives and souls. He's ready to turn back the battle at the gates.

So He picks the most difficult gates He can find. Jesus began His assault, as we have seen, at Caesarea Philippi, outside the shrine to the god Pan where the 'Gates of Hell' were located. There a name exchange occurred— 'Messiah' from Simon, 'Cephas', *cornerstone*, from Jesus. Simon, now called 'Peter' or 'Cephas' has become the founding member of the church. What is the church and what is its mission statement? Well, the modern Hebrew equivalent of 'ekklesia' is 'knesset'—which is the name for the Israeli parliament.[105]

The church is thus God's government. This is made clear when Jesus says '*whatever you bind on earth shall have been bound in heaven, and whatever you loose on earth shall have been loosed in heaven.*' (Matthew 16:19 NAS) The words for *bind* and *loose* refer to the making of laws: creating legal injunctions, prohibiting certain activities, annulling particular decrees and so on.

Jesus began with a name covenant with Simon. But a new name covenant, by itself, is vulnerable, exposed, at great risk. When God begins to talk to you about His own name and yours, offering you a name exchange, the enemy will instantly turn his attention to you and zoom in for an attack. It's no coincidence that Jesus calls Simon Peter 'blessed' one moment and, right on its heels, rebukes him with 'Get behind Me, Satan!'[106]

The moment God starts talking name covenant with you, the satan's dossier on the possibilities within your name narrows to a superfine focus. Your destiny is now up in lights. Clear for the entire spiritual realm to see. This is one of the reasons why God offers a threshold covenant so quickly afterwards: to protect what has just been conceived.

With a threshold covenant, God arrives as covenant defender. For Peter, as the founding member of God's government, it occurred when he was taken with James and John up a high mountain to witness Jesus being transfigured in glory. This mountain is, I believe, Mount Hermon—where the seventy sons of the supreme Canaanite god had their palace—that is, their seat of government. It is no coincidence that, on coming back down the mountain, one of His first actions is to send out seventy disciples.

(P. 55, 69)

Seventy, throughout Scripture, is the number which symbolises world government. Jesus set Himself against the principalities which had invaded Israel—the land God had set aside for Himself and His chosen people—and began to establish His Kingdom, a kingdom not of this world.

Nearly six centuries previously, Daniel had prayed to heaven and, although the answer was sent at once, it took twenty-one days before the angel Gabriel was able to get through to him. During that time Gabriel had battled in the heavenlies and had only been successful in getting past the opposition when Michael joined him to fight the prince of Persia. This prince was almost certainly Mitra, *lord of the contract*, who by the time of the Romans had become the Mithras who laid claim to the titles, '*The Light of the World*' and '*Invincible Sun*'.

Jesus is the 'Sun of Righteousness' (and yes, it is 'sun' not 'son') who rises with healing in His wings. This metaphor, 'wings', refers to the ends of prayer shawl—the 'tallit' worn by observant Jews. On the hem of the wings were knotted fringes, called 'tzitzit', which were fingered during prayer. When people came to Jesus, begging to touch the hem of His garment, they were actually asking to take hold of His prayer life, to be joined with Him as He interceded before the Father. No wonder they were all healed!

Today, instead of going to this same place by faith, instead of being humbly aware that without Jesus we can do nothing, there's a tendency to rely on our own authority and to cross the line from faith to magic. When we decree and declare things that are out of alignment with God's will, we are practising magic. When we deliberately ignore God's Word and then pray the covering of the blood of Jesus over our defiance in an attempt to nullify the consequence, we are practising magic. I am thinking here of numerous people who suffer terrible retaliation because, although they know that both Jude 1:8–11 and 2 Peter 2:10–15 warn against cursing, reviling and abusing dark angelic princes, do it anyway! They consider those verses don't apply to them because they regard themselves as having authority that supersedes those Scriptures!

An increasingly common practice is 'trading'—and, in many cases, the motive for participating in it is questionable. If we use trading as a solution to our material and financial problems, we're simply trying to buy divine favour. It's all too easy to cross the line and indulge in tricks similar to those that resulted in the satan's expulsion from heaven. Trying to trade with God—making a small financial investment in the hope of a greatly multiplied return—misunderstands relationship. Offering Him sacrifices of praise and thanksgiving and firstfruits and tithes—a portion of what He has given us in order to express our gratitude and willingness to acknowledge His first place in our lives—yes, that's repeatedly stressed. But trading is not—and I believe that's for a very simple reason: it's a short half-step to the cliff plunging into the abyss.

Yes, Jesus did do a trade on the cross: sin for righteousness. However, this is an integral part of His offer of blood covenant to us. Overall, many current practises are the result of a failure to trust God and to understand His grace, His rest and the undeserved exchanges of covenant.

Desperate circumstances do not require trading—desperate circumstances require confession, repentance and forgiveness. When faith is expressed as trading, we have lost ourselves. Faith is that crumb of hope that causes us to lay hold of the hem of Jesus' prayer shawl and believe that His intercession before the Father is enough.

Yes, He does indeed call us to the task of offering our names back to Him as their true owner. And yes, there will be an exchange—but only as part of a covenant. And what makes a covenant different to a trade or a contract?

It's simple. As we noted before: it's oneness. When we exchange names, we say: 'It's no longer "me" and "me", but "we". Like the father in the story of the Prodigal Son, our heavenly Father says to us, '*Everything I have is yours.*' (Luke 15:31 NIV) Yet suddenly, instead of trusting in the benefits of sonship, we fall for the temptation of reverting to a business relationship.

Let us not sell our inheritance, as Esau did, for some red.

Name covenants are an invitation to friendship. When the proposal comes from God, it necessarily involves threshold covenant and this means He is also offering to become our covenant defender. Now, make no mistake about it, God as our armour-bearer, as our battle partner and as our divine defender is the most awesome privilege. All our worries are over, right?

No.

Being a 'friend of God' means that we've passed quite a few tests, but there are still very tough ones to come. When His promises threaten to become more important than Himself, God may ask us to sacrifice them. When our destiny supplants the Lord in our lives, He may require the gift back—as, for instance, He asked of Abraham with respect to Isaac.

Passing such a test is not a foregone conclusion. Simon Peter choked on his test—failing so badly that he threw in the towel and went back to his old profession of fishing.[107] Jesus gently restored him: a fire at dawn on a threshold and three affirmations of his destiny in order to counter his three denials around a fire on another threshold.

Paul also, in my opinion, fell flat on his face when confronted with a threshold test. Yes, I know that it's an almost universal view that when Paul and Silas were in Philippi it was a triumph all the way. But just as Peter's test involved his name and his destiny—Cephas, *the cornerstone, the threshold* and a whole battery of poetically related words in Hebrew such as *doorway, palm of the hand, servant girl, garden, rooster,* not to mention Caiaphas—so too Paul's test revolves around his own name.

Paul and Silas were in prison at Philippi, having been thrown there by the local magistrates. They'd caused a whole heap of trouble by delivering a slave girl of a Python spirit. Now they were praying and singing hymns when, around midnight, an earthquake occurred. All the prison doors flew open and the prisoners' chains fell off. The jailer was sure that everyone had escaped and was about to kill himself to escape summary execution when Paul called out to him.

'What must I do to be saved?' the jailer asked—rounding off a story which began with the deliverance of a slave girl and goes on to finish with the salvation of an entire family.

Now, despite the all-things-work-together-for-good ending, I don't think that Paul thought this was the best outcome. As I've pointed out in *Dealing with Python,* I think he knew he'd made a huge mistake—a mistake that cost him his ministry in Philippi. He was forced to leave town the very next day. I also think the words within the story itself indicate Paul was aware of the test: words like *judge, pray, deliver, escape, tremble, earthquake.* In Hebrew, these are all inter-related and they sound like they come from 'Paul'.

The word for *earthquake* is 'peleg' related to 'palats', *tremble*, and to 'pallatsuth', *shuddering*. The figure of Justice, symbolised by a set of quivering scales, shows the probable relationship between these words and 'palal', *judge, pray, intercede, entreat*[108] and well as 'palat', *deliver* or *escape*—since a judge's verdict can be a means of deliverance.

All these various elements—prayer, intercession, judgment, earthquake, deliverance—combine in a single story shot through with threshold covenant overtones. And it is indeed a threshold, not simply because of the explicit mention of the spirit of Python in the story, but because the preaching of the gospel is in the process of transitioning between continents: from Asia to Europe. It's my belief that Paul knew he'd muffed the test—and that, later, when confronted with Python again, he'd realised the nature of his mistake. As I point out in *Dealing with Python*, it's all too easy to make the same mistake as Paul did and think that faith—*more* faith—will overcome this spirit. But, as Paul recognised by the time he wrote to the Corinthians, faith isn't the answer. It's love.

To overcome the threshold spirits who want to strip us of the new name covenant we've received—or trade with us, giving us ashes for beauty—we need a whole garden of aromatic fruit and flowers. We need love to overcome Python, the spirit of constriction; and joy to overcome Ziz, the spirit of forgetting; and peace to overcome Leviathan, the spirit of retribution; and patience to overcome Rachab, the spirit of wasting. Yes, this is one of the purposes of the fruit of the Spirit: to help us cross the threshold. Just as David got out his slingshot and whirled a stone at Goliath, we've got to get out our slingshot, toss in a pebble of joy and fling it at Ziz.

But we also need armour. The armour of God is specifically designed for crossing thresholds. We can be sure of that because seven words for parts of the threshold are encoded in Ephesians 6:12–20. Seven allusions to flowers are also encoded there: pomegranate, anenome, manna, mustard, lily, rose of Sharon, almond.[109]

The flowers and the fruit should remind us of a garden. Yes, in name covenant, God is calling us back to the Garden, to the intimacy of Eden, before oneness was broken.

In blood covenant, God calls us home. He hugs us, surrounding us with family, and sings over us with a Daddy's delight. But in name covenant, He invites us into friendship. And with threshold covenant, He starts to share His secrets, asks us to join His council, selects us to become part of His government, summons us to judge angels and tests us to the limit. But He also promises, so long as we keep covenant with Him, to defend us to the death and lavish our long-lost inheritance on us.

It's wondrous. It's challenging. It's scary. It's honouring.

I hope that, today, you choose to go forward into it. Because it's what you were made for.

All names in heaven and on earth come from God. *All* names. Every single name we've ever been known by, including our nicknames. But until we ask God to make holy His name within our own names—to consecrate it and set it apart for Himself—the name remains in the hands of the enemy. Jesus has shown us the way. Let us take hold of His prayer tassels and unite ourselves to the renaming He has already accomplished. For through that renaming, He has made it possible for our identities, our destinies and our callings to be returned to us.

Let us glorify His name as we answer His summons into that destiny.

Great Heavenly Father, YHWH,

I come before you today, clinging to the tassels of Yahushua's prayer shawl, so that He may interceed for me. I thank you for your plan of salvation, to redeem us through the innocent shed blood of the Messiah.

My desire is to love you more and to know You more.

My prayer is that My Elohim would show me how to grow closer and to love more deeply so that I can become a friend to You YHWH and Yahushua. I ask You to make Holy Your name with my name or a new name for me, through a name covenant, and to protect

me from the enemy.
I also ask that you
protect Jennifer & Lothar
from the enemy and dark
angels who seek to corrupt
their spiritual longing for
You. Please shed your love
and your truth in their lives
and prevent the enemy
from attacking them to get
at me and prevent me
from being part of your
glorious kingdom. I would
like to extend my prayer of
protection to my mom, Brenda
and Anna. For, I know that
they love you.
Blessings and peace
and honour, my dear
Elohim - love Barbara

Appendix 1

Summary

A name covenant involves, first and foremost, an exchange of names. In many places throughout the world, the covenant also involves an understanding that those involved in the exchange are adopted into each other's family.

Name covenants have been going on for thousands of years. Culturally, they have been practised—particularly throughout Oceania—until the mid-twentieth century. Famous people of recent centuries who participated in them include Captain James Cook, Robert Louis Stevenson, Paul Gauguin, Governor Arthur Phillip, Woollarawarre Bennelong, Lieutenant William Clark.

Scriptural examples of name covenants fall into two categories: those between two human beings and those where one of the partners is divine. When name covenant involves God, there are three standard components to the event:

1. The usual name exchange, which testifies to the oneness of the partners through saying, in effect, 'It's no longer "I" but "we".'

2. A revelation of a new—or hidden—divine name.

3. A new name for the human partner which involves a poetic tweak or a re-definition or a replacement.

Examples of 'tweaks' are names like Abram to Abraham, Sarai to Sarah, Saul to Paul, Hosea to Joshua.

Examples of replacement are Simon to Cephas (or Peter), Jacob to Israel.

Examples of re-definitions are Gideon or Mary Magdalene. This last one is, quite possibly, an unusual example of God accepting human initiative when it comes to name covenant. In all other instances, it would appear He was the one proposing the exchange.

It is not compulsory to accept a name covenant with God. It appears that God offered Moses a name exchange with covenantal blessings at Mount Sinai. He made this proposal by revealing a previously unknown name for Himself—*I AM WHO I AM*—and also suggesting to Moses a minor modification for his own name.[110] Despite repeated chances over the next forty years, Moses seems to have consistently refused this offer.

A name exchange is extremely significant in its own right. It is an invitation to friendship. However, as far as divine covenants go, it is a prelude to a threshold covenant. There's no point in one without the other—the first is the gift of a new identity and destiny. The second is the invitation to pass through the doorway into that destiny. These two covenants are normally separated by six days in Scripture. They are, respectively, the second and third of the covenants God wants to give us.

The first is blood covenant which gives us status as a Child of God, the second is name covenant which offers an invitation to become a Friend of God, the third is threshold covenant, the fourth is salt covenant and the fifth is covenant of peace. With blood covenant, we receive the blessings of covenant but Jesus has taken the curses on Himself on the Cross. With name covenant, we are in a position of responsibility. The curses will fall on us if we betray God's friendship. This is the consistent message of Scripture where the great reversals of the nation happen after this kind of covenant violation.

Testing follows re-naming. These tests can take either of two forms:

1. Those that give an opportunity to pass previously failed tests, such as Abraham going to Gerar to re-do the test he failed in Egypt. However, in saying that Sarah was his sister, not his wife, he failed a second time.

2. Those that give an opportunity to choose God as our identity—and not succumb to the temptation to place our identity in our destiny. An example of this kind of test is that of God asking Abraham to sacrifice Isaac.

When we fail the tests, we forfeit the testimony we might otherwise have had. More than that, however, more than sacrificing an opportunity to praise and glorify God through becoming an overcomer, we leave the problem for our children to solve. We also make it worse for them because we've role-modelled failure, not success—and also because, spiritually speaking, the longer a problem goes on, the more enlarged and entrenched it becomes. 'Sow the wind, reap the whirlwind,' says Hosea 8:7—an expression of the spiritual law of multiplication.

The satan mimics name covenants, trading with us for them and for the calling that comes with them. Jesus constantly claimed names and titles back from the satan during His ministry. However, we are often in agreement with the satan's claim. There are two kinds of agreement: the first is due to ignorance and is by default—because we don't know of the existence of a name covenant, we simply don't do anything about revoking it. We just let it lie. The second kind of agreement is an active agreement when we say things like: 'Easter comes from the name of a pagan goddess.' This does not acknowledge that ultimately the name was stolen from the Father who is the giver of all names in heaven and on earth.

God still offers name covenants, even in the present day and age. The satan still demands name trades, even in the present day and age. In my experience, both covenants and trades follow the old established rules.

Name covenants are one of the lost signposts along the ancient paths that point to a wider spiritual scope in Jesus' reclamation of seven of the names of God.

Appendix 2

Name Covenants in Scripture

The following list highlights people mentioned in Scripture who had an obvious name covenant, *or* alternatively very likely had one *or* who were offered one.

1. Abednego, also called Azariah
2. Abram, also called Abraham
3. Daniel, also called Belteshazzar
4. Eliakim, also called Jehoakim
5. Esau, also called Edom
6. Gideon, also called Jerub-Baal
7. Hadassah, also called Esther
8. Hoshea, also called Joshua
9. Jacob, also called Israel.
10. Jesus, also called Lamb of God, also called Son of God, Son of Man, Son of David, Son of Joseph, Messiah or Christ, Master, Logos or The Word, Root and Offspring of David, Light of the World, Bread Come Down From Heaven, True Vine, Good Shepherd, Door of the Sheep, The Way, the Truth and the Life, The Resurrection and the Life, Chief Cornerstone, Bright and Morning Star, Second Adam.
11. John, also called a Son of Thunder

12. Jonathan, also called Jehonathan
13. Joseph, also called Zaphenath-Paneah
14. Joseph, also called Barnabas
15. Mary, also called Magdalene
16. Meshach, also called Mishael
17. Moses, offered the name Mazzah
18. Phinehas, also called Pinchas
19. Sarai, also called Sarah
20. Saul, also called Paul
21. Sergius Paulus, who probably exchanged names with Saul
22. Shadrach, also called Hananiah
23. Simon also called Peter, also called Cephas
24. Solomon, also called Jedidiah
25. Zedekiah, also known as Mattaniah

The following list includes people mentioned in Scripture who were known by more than one name but about whom there is insufficient information to decide whether a name covenant is likely.

1. Ahasuerus, also called Artaxerxes
2. Ater, also called Hezekiah
3. Bar-Jesus, also called Elymas the sorcerer
4. Bartholomew, also called Nathanael
5. John, also called Mark
6. Josheb-Basshebetha, also called Adino the Eznite
7. Joseph, also called Barsabbas, also called Justus
8. Joshua, also called Justus
9. Kelaiah, also called Kelita
10. Simeon, also called Niger
11. Thomas, also called Didymus
12. Tiglath-Pileser, also called Pul

The following are places with more than one name:

1. Beersheba, also called Sheba
2. Bela, also called Zoar
3. Dor, also called Napoth Dor
4. Edom, also called Seir
5. En Mispat, also called Kadesh
6. Ephrath, also called Bethlehem, also called Ephrathah
7. Gederah, also called Gederothaim
8. Hazazon Tamar, also called En Gedi
9. Holy Tent, also called Meeting Tent
10. House of the Lord, also called Temple
11. Jebus, also called Jerusalem
12. Kerioth Hezron, also called Hazor
13. Kiriath Arba, also called Hebron, also called Mamre
14. Kiriath Baal, also called Kiriath Jearim, also called Baalah of Judah
15. Kiriath Sannah, also called Debir
16. Laish, also called Leshem, also called Dan
17. Luz, also called Bethel
18. Mizpah, also called Galeed
19. Moab, also called Ar
20. Mount Jearim, also called Kesalon
21. Mount Sirion, also called Hermon, also called Senir
22. Sea of Galilee, also called Sea of Tiberias
23. Throne Room, also called the Hall of Judgment
24. Valley of Shaveh, also called King's Valley

Appendix 3

Remembering Names

How many times have you been totally in the zone and intently focussed on an activity when—suddenly—you're jolted out of it by an awareness someone nearby has just used your own name? 'Did you get all that?' someone may then ask you about some important news being discussed just a few steps away. And you have to admit, 'No,' because your attention was totally elsewhere until your name popped up.

Even as infants we recognise our own names. Specific activity occurs in babies' brains when names are spoken; this cerebral activity is different from other words.

Now of course all this should come as no surprise, since names are so significant throughout Scripture. In the first book of the Bible, the first gift given to Adam—after that of life itself—is the right to gift names. In the last book of the Bible, the first new thing God promises us is a new *name*.

God is big on names. Your name—and that of other people—are incredibly important to Him. It's all too easy to think 'I'm hopeless with names,' and excuse yourself from any effort to change. Remember that every name in heaven and on earth comes from the Father so, in recalling the names of other people, you are ultimately using one of His names.

So here are some simple and helpful ways to recall names:

1. If you're on the phone, repeat the person's name, jot it down and—even if you're only contacting a business to make an inquiry—when you're finished, thank the person by name.

2. If you're meeting in person, say, 'Pleased to meet you,' and immediately use their name. Make sure you have the right pronunciation by repeating it back after them.

3. Use the person's name during any conversation so it has a chance to sink in.

4. Reaching out to someone in order to introduce them to Jesus means caring enough to remember their name. It tells the other person that you consider them important and that God values them. It's said the sweetest sound in any language is your own name, so make an effort to cultivate the skill of remembering names.

Appendix 4

Naming For Unresolved Family Issues

Yes, it happens all the time. Even today. Parents prayerfully choose a name for a child—only to come up with a word that spells out the major unresolved issue of their family line. What they are actually doing is prophesying that the child is called to resolve that issue. But this is a family business, not the child's task alone. By putting the problem front and centre—by naming it every time the child is called to breakfast, to clean up, to get ready for school—the parents should also be praying to support the child in healing the ancestral bloodline. Because the children are the ones now facing the tests everyone else has failed. They are the chosen ones for their generation. Make no mistake, they *cannot* 'make up' for the failures of the past—only Jesus can do that. However, they can be overcomers and restorers.

Scriptural examples of people naming their children for unresolved issues include Isaac who named his son Jacob, *deceiver*, for the unresolved family issue of deceit. Abram had deceived Pharaoh over his relationship with Sarai and later, even when he'd been renamed Abraham and had four covenants with God, he did not pass the repeat test when he went to Gerar. There he deceived Abimelech in the same way and, in a later generation, so did Isaac in the matter of Rebekah.

The unresolved issue for Joseph was his mother's death. He named his second son Ephraim, *doubly fruitful*; however the word is related to the name of the place where Rachel died: Ephrathah in the vicinity of Bethlehem.

Gideon names his son Abimelech, *my father is king*. Gideon himself refused the offer of kingship but it would seem there may well have been unresolved feelings there because Abimelech kills all but one of his seventy brothers to make sure he got what his father had turned down.

David names his sons Absalom, *my father is peace*, and Solomon, *man of peace*, for the unresolved family issue of war. The family comes from Bethlehem, usually given as meaning *house of bread* but also meaning *house of war*. (Yes, there's more than one word for *war* in Hebrew.) The ongoing war between the people of Bethlehem and the people of Gibeah is only truly and finally resolved by Jesus on the day of His resurrection.[111] It is because David is a '*man of war*' who has shed blood that God does not give him permission to build the Temple. (1 Chronicles 28:3)

David has an uncle Jonathan and a nephew Jonathan. Saul's son is Jonathan. In both families, the unresolved issue is hatred of a man named Jonathan—who happened to be the grandson of Moses. His actions following the rape and murder of his concubine at Gibeah were the flashpoint which ignited the centuries-long war between the people of Bethlehem and those of Gibeah. Saul wasn't simply jealous of David because of the praise he received—his hatred was fuelled by the generational feud between the men of Gibeah and the men of Bethlehem.

Jonathan (also called Jehonathan), son of Saul, did much to repair the breach, which was often to engulf the entire nation. However, only through the actions of Jesus on the road to Emmaus was this dark episode of history truly and gloriously healed.

Appendix 5

Oath Brothers

'Eida broda.'

When I write books like this, I always finish a draft and then pray God will remind me of anything I've missed so I can include it during the next edit. So when I completed the last draft, I thought I was done.

However, as I woke up the next morning, two clearly articulated words echoed through the foggy half-haze between sleep and full consciousness: 'Eida broda.'

I had no idea what that meant. Was it a bubble of ancestral memory surfacing from deep within? Was it perhaps the tail-end of a dream? Or, was it a message from the gates of heaven? I've had this kind of experience more than once over the years and, at first, I dismissed such events as random bits of sleep flotsam. But over time I've learned not to ignore them.

Still, revelations like this are usually problematic. Phrases that are clearly in foreign languages unfortunately don't ever come with spelling attached. And finding the meaning of the phrase is critically dependent on getting the spelling right. Happily, this particular phrase sounded

Teutonic, maybe even Old Norse. That meant I had a reasonably decent chance of approximating the correct spelling—which wouldn't be the case if it were Gaelic or even one of the Romance languages.

A quarter hour with Google and I decided the correct spelling was probably 'eiðr bróðir', the first word meaning *oath* and the second meaning *brother*. Together they make 'eið-bróðir', *oath brother*.

This refers to pairs of men or even entire brotherhoods who had sworn blood oaths to one another. They'd become brothers, though unrelated, they considered themselves kin with all the obligations of family towards one another. Now while I can find no instances of name covenanting in this regard, I don't want to overlook the practice either. It is clearly a close relative of the Hebrew blood covenant, since it involves the ritualistic mingling of blood and, most importantly of all, the understanding that lives become a single unity through that mingling.

The Anglo-Saxon word that most closely approximates covenant is 'wǽr' which has a general meaning of *pledge*, *compact*, *agreement*, *covenant*. It was connected with betrothal which, of course, is about not just a couple joining together in matrimony to become one, but also their respective families joining into a new relationship.

This word 'wǽr' also had a connotation of *truth*. Related to the Latin 'ver', this sense survives in the modern word 'verity', *truth*. In addition 'wǽr' survives in 'warlock' which, while it has overtones of sorcery and the occult today, originally simply meant *oath-breaker* or *covenant-violator* or *liar against the truth*. (While it might seem from 'warlock' that 'war'—as in 'warfare'—is derived also from 'wǽr', that is said not to be the case. Instead, 'war' allegedly comes from 'werre', a word meaning *confusion* or *mixture*. So the humble sausage—'wurst'—is closely related to 'war' in concept, but 'warlock' is not!)

The word 'wǽr' translated into Norse is 'var' and can be found in one of the most famous of all military brotherhoods: the Varangian Guard. For four centuries, an elite unit of crack warriors, initially from the Rus tribe—Norsemen living in Sweden who gave their name to Russia—served the emperor of Constantinople. Apparently recognisable by their long hair, a ruby set in their left ear and ornamental dragons sewn on their chainmail shirts, they formed the Byzantine emperor's personal bodyguard. Despite their mercenary status, their loyalty was unquestionable and legendary—but, in this, they simply kept the long-standing Germanic tradition that oath-bound service meant 'faithful unto death'. Many Northmen, including Anglo-Saxons in later centuries, made their fortunes serving for a time in the Varangian Guard.

By the fourteenth century, Byzantium was waning as a power in the Middle East. As a consequence, the era of the Varangian Guard came to an end. And it is perhaps no coincidence that oath-bound service took on an entirely different slant in the rising Ottoman Empire, where a new kind of bodyguard came to prominence: the Janissaries. Wikipedia says: 'They began as an elite corps of slaves made up of kidnapped young Christian boys who were forcefully converted to Islam, and became famed for internal cohesion cemented by strict discipline and order. Unlike typical slaves, they were paid regular salaries.

Forbidden to marry or engage in trade, their complete loyalty to the Sultan was expected.' They were considered 'kapikullari' or *a door servant*, that is, *a slave of the Porte*.

The stark contrast between the submission of the Varangians and that of the Janissaries could not be more evident. The first were freemen offering covenant-like loyalty for as long as their service lasted. The second were slaves brainwashed into total obedience. The spiritual significance of the latter is evident in the designation: *door servant*.

There is a spirit of armies which is a threshold guardian. Like the Janissaries who were indoctrinated to fight against their own people, their own homeland and their own fathers, this spirit is so opposed to the 'father' it wouldn't think twice about killing him. Failing that, it wants to destroy all the 'father' stands for: including, in our time, the foundation of a Christian society with all that that entails.

The agreements that come down family lines through ungodly name covenants or threshold covenants cause us immense problems. Many of these agreements are ones that, if we knew about them, we'd be horrified. And if that's the case, then we should realise we've come to this point in our lives as conditioned and enslaved as Janissaries. Opposed to our heavenly Father because we are unknowingly loyal to His enemy.

A spiritually-mixed covenant is the work of demons, not the work of the Father. It makes us 'wǽrloga'—*warlocks*— that is, *covenant-breakers, truth-violators*. God declines to be involved in something so unholy. And while in His love and grace and mercy, He still stands in harm's way for us, it is not the same as the covenant defence He offers us when we renounce our complicity with the enemy and turn fully and completely to Him.

Covenants are forever. They have no end-date, no termination clause, no let-out condition. They involve family lines forever. Complicity with unholy covenants may be active or it may be passive—it may involve nothing more than shrugging our shoulders, deciding it's all too hard and leaving it for someone else to deal with. But in every generation the problem gets worse.

It's not just individuals that God wants to summon into a high calling and matchless destiny, it's also families.

When we purify our name covenant, it applies to more than ourselves.

Appendix 6

Model Prayers

Unbelief

'What can I do to make this right?' That's our heart's cry regarding name covenants and thresholds. This question points to the single most significant issue of unbelief concerning the threshold: the atonement of Jesus on the cross. Jesus is the all-sufficient sacrifice to enable us to cross the threshold—but some part of our hearts not only *won't* believe this but *can't* believe it. We are totally resistant to the thought that there's nothing—absolutely nothing—we can add to the atonement. And worst of all, we don't know we're resistant. We deny our own unbelief. Even when we discern the denial and try to repent of our attitude, it's only to find the unbelief springs back, more resilient than ever. How can it be that there is nothing we can do about our own collaboration with the enemy? Can't we 'do' something—like confess? Or repent? Or forgive? Our hearts can't believe that even repentance is not from us. We can want to repent but we can't achieve it. We can want to forgive, but we can never accomplish it on our own. All we can 'do' is acknowledge we can't do anything:

Father, I come by faith before Your throne

in order to confess that am resistant to repentance.

I want to add to the atonement of Jesus. I know intellectually I can't do it but my heart holds out the necessity of doing something to make it avail for me. My heart keeps telling me there is something undone that I have to do to make it complete. All I can 'do' is say the words: 'I repent of not believing that the blood of Jesus is sufficient.'

Father, I call on Jesus as my mediator and I ask Him to empower this declaration of repentance and break down my resistance through His blood. I declare here on earth and in any and every spiritual realm, before the heavens and in the highest heaven, as well as for all time, that I am no longer in agreement with my unbelief about the atonement. But I admit this declaration is just hot air unless the atoning blood of Jesus actually empowers it.

I therefore ask Your grace to cut through to me—I'm caught in the trap where I need to believe in the atonement so that the atonement can be effective. However I can't overcome my unbelief in order for that to happen. My unbelief is too strong for me to cut it off myself. It's also too mixed and adulterated with faith for me to even know where to begin separating the two. So I throw myself on Your mercy and ask You to do in me what I can't do for myself. I ask for the atonement to be made real in me and to me.

I join my voice with that of the centurion who came to Jesus: 'Lord, I believe. Help my unbelief.'

And, Lord, I ask this prayer to be granted through the power of the atoning blood of Jesus and in His name.

Purification of a Name

This prayer should be used as a guideline, not as a formula. It is one of several prayers found in the appendices of *God's Pottery*, to deal with different issues surrounding the threshold.

Father in heaven, I would like to cut a name covenant with You but I await Your direction and timing for it. In the meantime, please come as the refiner and place my name in your crucible of purification. Gently apply the fire of Your Holy Spirit to my name so all impurity is bubbled out. As each defilement over my name rises to the surface, please skim it off.

Father, please work over my name seven times, as You would a crucible of silver, until such time as You can see Your own face reflected in it. May Your crucible hold each part of my name, each letter, each syllable, each arrangement of letters and syllables, every elision between words, every nickname, workcode, pen-name, pet-name, name before birth or name before marriage.

Father, I give my name into Your keeping. If any spirit claims ownership of it, please deny that claim in Your court. If my heart is in hidden dispute with You about my name, please remind it of Ephesians 3:15–16, that You are *'the Father, from whom every family in heaven and on earth is named.'* When You are ready, please return to me dominion of the gift You gave to Adam—that of naming— and cut a name covenant with me. I ask this in the name of Him who is the Name above all names, Jesus of Nazareth.

Amen

Appendix 7

Further Reading

God's Pottery—The Sea of Names and the Pierced Inheritance

The name covenant between El Shaddai and Abraham is the first *explicit* name covenant in the Bible. The first *implicit* one is hidden in Genesis 1:1. *God's Pottery* (which should ideally be read after *God's Pageantry*) explores the wonder of this name particular covenant and explains the reason why the time period between name and threshold covenant is six days.

God's Poetry—The Identity and Destiny Encoded in Your Name

The title says it all. God is a poet and He breathes into you both identity and your calling at conception when He gives you a soul. A look at some of the famous names of the Bible and how the poetry of their names affected their destiny—both positively and negatively.

The Threshold Covenant: The Beginning of Religious Rites ~ Henry Clay Trumbull

Originally published at the end of the nineteenth century, this book is readily available online in various formats.

A wonderful introduction to the basics of threshold covenant, its practice, its history and its significance.

Supernatural ~ Michael S Heiser

The Unseen Realm ~ Michael S Heiser

Supernatural is the 'lite' version of *The Unseen Realm,* which has a very academic flavour. Heiser's view of the spiritual world as described in these books and in *Reversing Hermon* is, of all authors I have ever read, the one closest to my own. There isn't much on covenant in these books, and nothing at all on name covenants. I am recommending them for their exposition of the way heaven operates. Heiser came to his views through a hard-core intellectual encounter with Psalm 82; I came to mine through a troubled time in my life when God told me the answer to my problems lay in that same psalm.

Needless Casualties of War ~ John Paul Jackson

So many people get smashed because they ignore Scriptural principles and protocols for battle or for court. We can't simply assume that God will protect us because of our ignorance. This book points out some of the common practices of churches today that are actually in violation of God's Word.

Many people have asked me to write on salt and blood covenant. But I think others have done it far better than I ever could. There are many fine articles about blood covenant on the internet. So let me just suggest you go searching, with a single warning: ultimately covenant is about *oneness*, while contract is about exchange. The covenant ceremony has exchanges; but to focus on the swapping and trading is to miss the most significant point. The exchanges are to symbolise and to emphasise the *oneness* committed to in the pledges. Without that *oneness*, you just have a contract. Bearing this difference between contract and covenant in mind—because it tends to get lost in many explanations, let me recommend regarding the salt covenant:

The Covenant of Salt: As Based on the Significance and Symbolism of Salt in Primitive Thought ~ Henry Clay Trumbull

Again, a much older book from the nineteenth century, readily available online.

The Covenant of Salt ~ John Loren Sandford

An audio CD which details the practice and application of the covenant of salt.

Endnotes

1. *Selected Letters of Robert Louis Stevenson*, ed. Ernest Mehew, Yale University Press 2001

2. A letter from Fanny Stevenson to Sidney Colvin, written from Tautira in December 1888, recounts Stevenson's exchange of names with Ori a Ori, and in doing so conveys her family's understanding of the significance of the act.

   Fanny states that her husband initiated the transaction, using Princess Moë to convey his request to Ori, who responded by offering 'brotherhood' to the foreign visitor. 'So now, if you please, Louis is no more Louis, having given that name away in the Tahitian form of Rui, but is known as Terii-Tera (pronounced Teree terah) that being Ori's Christian name. "Ori of Ori" is his clan name.'

   The material significance of the exchange was revealed when delays to repairs on their yacht at Papeete left the Stevensons reliant on Ori's extended hospitality: Then Ori of Ori, the magnificent, who listened to the tale of the shipwrecked mariners with serious dignity, asking [sic] one or two questions, and then spoke to this effect. 'You are my brother: all that I have is yours. I know that your food is done, but I can give you plenty of fish and taro. We like you, and wish to have you here. Stay where you are till the *Casco* comes. Be happy—*et ne pleurez pas.*' Louis dropped his head into his hands and wept, and then we all went up to Rui and shook hands with him and accepted his offer.

In Fanny's humorously hyperbolic account, Ori's injunction not to cry has the opposite effect, with the offer and its acceptance being accompanied by outpourings of emotion from all present. The following day, 'amidst a raging sea and a storming wind', Ori sailed to Papeete to collect European food supplies for the visitors, carrying letters of introduction which express Stevenson's sense of obligation to the man he described as his 'FRIEND and HOST'.

These letters, together with Fanny's account, demonstrate that the Stevensons regarded their bond with Ori as one of genuine friendship as well as formal kinship, a relationship in which sentiment, obligation and advantage were all combined. *The Song of Rahéro* begins with a verse dedication, six lines of unrhymed iambic pentameter addressed to Stevenson's 'brother':

Ori, my brother in the island mode,
In every tongue and meaning much my friend,
This story of your country and your clan,
In your loved house, your too much honoured guest,
I made in English. Take it, being done;
And let me sign it with the name you gave.

Teriitera

International Journal of Scottish Literature, http://www.ijsl.stir.ac.uk/issue9/jolly.pdf, accessed 29 March 2018

3. Also spelled 'tayo' or 'tyo'.

4. *International Journal of Scottish Literature*, http://www.ijsl.stir.ac.uk/issue9/jolly.pdf, accessed 29 March 2018

5. *International Journal of Scottish Literature*, http://www.

ijsl.stir.ac.uk/issue9/jolly.pdf accessed 29 March 2018

6. *Intimate Strangers: Friendship, Exchange and Pacific Encounters*, Vanessa Smith, Cambridge University Press 2010

7. *The Captain and His Book in the Victoria River Country, and Beyond*, Deborah Bird Rose, Macquarie University http://www.nla.gov.au/events/cooks-treasures/papers/Deborah-Rose-Captain-Cook.pdf accessed 31 March 2018

8. He was also called Tu-nui-ea-i-te-atua-i-Tarahoi Vaira'atoa Taina Pōmare I as well as Tu or Tinah or Outu, or more formally as Tu-nui-a'a-i-te-atua.

9. *Bligh*, Anne Salmond, Penguin 2011

10. books.publishing.monash.edu/apps/bookworm/view/Writing+Histories%3A+Imagination+and+Narration/142/xhtml/chapter06.html

11. www2.hawaii.edu/~dennisk/voyaging_chiefs/aka.html

12. www.jps.auckland.ac.nz/document/Volume_73_1964/Volume_73,_No._4/Shorter_communications:_Notes_on_bond-friendship_in_Tahiti,_by_Ben_R._Finney,_p_431_-_435/p1#note14

13. en.wikipedia.org/wiki/James_Hanna_(trader) accessed 5 April 2018

14. www.biographi.ca/en/bio/eda_nsa_12E.html

15. Such exchange of names amongst the Western tribes of North America created a ceremonial kinship between the persons concerned. However, one scholar—Rees—believes that, despite this custom,

the name Clark was given was not the chief's name but was in fact 'kim-ah-pawn', which he interprets as *come and smoke*. This name, he says, comes from the time Clark smoked with the Shoshones on August 20, 1805. lewisandclarkjournals.unl.edu/read/?_ xmlsrc=1805-08-17.xml#noten20081705, accessed 5 April 2018

16. www.lewis-clark.org/article/3212, accessed 5 April 2018

17. eos.kokugakuin.ac.jp/modules/xwords/entry. php?entryID=84 accessed 5 April 2018

18. The word 'damuna' meant *exchange* amongst the Eora people. The person with whom you exchanged your name (and in some Aboriginal societies therefore became your trading partner) was your 'damelian' (feminine 'damelabillia') or *namesake*. On the other hand, the pejorative term 'damunalung', *someone who refused to give*, was put into English by marine lieutenant William Dawes as *a churl*, which meant *a surly or unfriendly person*.

19. www.eorapeople.com.au/tag/name-exchange/, accessed 11 April 2018

20. *Brokers and boundaries: Colonial exploration in indigenous territory*, Tiffany Shellam, Maria Nugent, Shino Konishi, Allison Cadzow, ANU Press 2016

21. Francois Peron, *Voyages de decouvertes aux terres Australes*, Atlas, 1811

22. Newton Fowell was a midshipman of the First Fleet flagship HMS *Sirius* and he recorded Colebee's names as 'Gringerry Kibba Coleby', 'Gringerry', 'Goungarree'

(according to Robert Brown, 1803) or 'Congare' (according to Maroot the Elder, as told to Benjamin Bowen Carter, 1798). His name may have derived from the Sydney language words for *cuts in the chest*. According to David Collins, 'Kibba' from gibba, kibba or kebah, meant a *rock* or *stone*. It was a term used to indicate that a man's front tooth had been knocked out by a stone during initiation. Similarly, Daniel Southwell gave Colebee the name of 'Kebada Colby.' It is likely that Colebee's totem was the white-bellied sea eagle, *haliaetus leucogaster*. In a caption for one of his pictures, the convict artist Thomas Watling recorded the name of this bird as 'goo-le-be', *gulbi*. Colebee exchanged names with the Gweagal (Fire Clan) warrior Wárungin Wángubile Kólbi. To distinguish between the two, the latter was called 'Botany Bay Colebee' by the colonists since he came from the south shore of Botany Bay. dictionaryofsydney.org/entry/colebee, accessed 12 July 2018

23. Also known as Nanbaree, Nanbarrey, Nanbaray, Nanbarry, Nanbree, Nanbury and Nanbarry Bolderry Brockenbau.

24. Thomas Watling drew a picture of Carradah or Karrada who, according to him, belonged to the Booroobeerungal (Boorooberongal) tribe. Watling also drew a picture of 'Wearrung' who had exchanged names with a Mr Long. www.nhm.ac.uk/nature-online/art-nature-imaging/ collections/first-fleet/art-collection/ethnography.ds ml?sa=2&lastDisp=list&notes=true&beginIndex=49&, accessed June 2018

25. http://bonesinthebelfry.com/Rowley/Ref%2003%20 A%20Cameo%20of%20Captain%20Thomas%20

ROWLEY%20-%20Ian%20Ramage.pdf, accessed July 2018

26. *Bennelong: The coming in of the Eora* (Kangaroo Press 2001), also www.eorapeople.com.au/tag/name-exchange/

27. *Excursions in New South Wales, Western Australia, and Van Dieman's Land during the Years 1830, 1831, 1832, and 1833*, William Henry Breton

28. *Six Years' Residence in the Australian Provinces: Ending in 1839*, Esq. William Mann

29. *Under His Banner: Papers on the Missionary Work of Modern Times*, Henry William Tucker, SPCK, 1872

30. http://www.heritageaustralia.com.au/downloads/pdfs/%20Heritage%200610_Thomas%20Huxley.pdf, accessed May 2018

31. For example:

    • In 1888, Maino the chief of Tutu, who is a crocodile-man, as a sign of friendship exchanged names with one of us and on the strength of this on arriving in Saibai in 1898, the white man claimed to be a crocodile-man also, and in this assertion he was supported by Maino who happened to be present. The other crocodile-men at once acknowledged the fact and a few minutes after landing on the island a crocodile-man made a present of some coconuts and stated in doing so that he was a relative.

    Reports of the Cambridge Anthropological Expedition to Torres Straits:
    Volume 5, Sociology, Magic and Religion of the Western Islanders
    A.C. Haddon, W. H. R. Rivers, C. G. Seligmann, A. Wilkin

- Matthew Flinders met a captain of the Macassan fleet who had exchanged names: Pobasso with Yolngu-Wirrpanda.

www.nomadart.com.au/documents/Djalkiri_ProjectNotes.pdf

- 'This stately fellow came up to us in the most gentlemanly manner possible, stating that he was "berry good black fellow" and, as he had no card, he gave us his name: 'Tom Ugly'. Another young man, who had undergone similar rites, and rejoicing in the English appellation of 'Jack Larkins' also made his appearance. Both these gentlemen fetched in a supply of water, and then sat down to assist us with our meal. An elderly native, who called himself 'Mr. Mason', ran up to us in great haste, greeting the corporal with all the demonstrations of the most cordial friendship. This old man had exchanged names with Mason, as a proof of his brotherly feeling: a distinction amongst his tribe of which he was not a little proud. The name given in return was 'Mooloo', by which title Mason was generally known amongst the surrounding tribes.

www.enzb.auckland.ac.nz/document?wid=599&page=1&action=null

- From the Solomon Islands: 'A friendly reception given, and, as a further proof of cordiality, the Bishop and the chief exchanged names, and, on the occasional visits paid in subsequent voyages, the same kindly welcome was given.'

anglicanhistory.org/oceania/patteson/drummond1930/

32. Such an example of the attitude to what were termed 'private adoptions' (which were not considered in the least unusual) but were in fact name covenants by the First Peoples of the United States is as follows: 'The selection

of someone as a "particular friend" was a very serious matter, to last a lifetime. This was usually "symbolized by a complete exchange of clothing and sometimes of names as well. It lasted throughout life, binding the Indians at least, in loyalty to his special friend, and often it was the means of saving" a white man's life. This custom is reflected in the name of "Judd's Friend" which was applied to the great warrior Ostenaco; and it may be hazarded, too, that the devotion of Atta Kulla Kulla, to which Captain John Stuart owed his escape from the Fort Loudoun massacre, was an exhibition of Indian loyalty to a "special friend". Both Ostenaco and Attakullakulla were from the Cherokee nation. Basically this kind of friendship points to the 'blood brother' concept [perhaps more currently rendered 'oath brother'] which, as the Manataka American Indian Council points out, seems to have dropped into obscurity: 'This seems to point to a custom which has escaped the notice of earlier writers on the eastern tribes, but which is well known in Africa and other parts of the world, and is closely analogous to a still existing ceremony among the plains Indians. By which two young men of the same tribe formally agree to become brothers, and ratify the compact by a public exchange of names and gifts.' www.manataka.org/page83.html, accessed 30 June 2018

33. In fact, we miss that the words of the hymn repeatedly express different aspects of covenant. They imply name exchange, weapon exchange, mantle exchange, and the oneness of spirit that comes with covenant—even the refuge that ensures we don't turn away into false covenant.

34. Perhaps derived from Hebrew, 'nakal', *wily*, *crafty*, *deceitful*, *tricky* or 'nakah', *conquer* via *smite*, *wound*,

defeat, *destroy* or 'nakeh', *crippled*

35. For example, Eliakim, son of Josiah, was renamed Jehoiakim by Pharaoh Necho when he made him king of Jerusalem and Judah in place of Jehoahaz (2 Kings 23:34 and 2 Chronicles 36:4)

36. *Isaiah's Vision and the Family of God*, Katheryn Pfisterer Darr, Westminster John Knox Press, 1994

37. It's unclear whether Abraham actually does that. However, his contemporary Job certainly does. The divine title 'El Shaddai' is frequently used in the book of Job

38. And as the Cree people say of identical twins.

39. A quote often attributed to John Keats.

40. There's an illuminating discussion on the names Abram and Abraham at the *Abarim Publications* website worth exploring. Although the 'rhm' overlap referring to covenant-cutting is noted there, it is considered too 'poetic' to be likely. However poetry is precisely why I think it is.

41. However, there's more to it than this. Let's play around with some of the Hebrew letters of Abraham's name: abrhm. With them we can make words corresponding to these English forms:

    - *Ebru* meaning *Hebrew*—a significant word in that Abraham was the first man to be known as a Hebrew.

    - *Arba* meaning *Hebron*—a significant word in that Abraham made his name covenant with God at Hebron, *passage*, which was originally called

Arba, *four*

- Barah meaning *covenant*—a significant word related to *blessing*, spelling out the prophetic destiny of Abraham as a blessing to all peoples through the cutting of this covenant

42. Similar to a nickname; an endearment.

43. See *God's Priority: World-Mending and Generational Testing* for details.

44. His younger brother, Ithamar, had a grandson Phinehas. This is spelled two different ways (1 Samuel 2:34, spelled פנחס only in 1 Samuel 1:3). This second Phinehas is the reprobate son of Eli, the priest of Shiloh. Perhaps there are hints of a name covenant in 1 Samuel 1:3 where his name is uniquely spelled without the 'yod' that characterises it afterwards. Certainly, another possible clue about a name covenant exists in this same verse: a new name of the Lord is revealed for the first time— Yahweh Sabaoth, *the Lord of Hosts.*

45. This is by no means a new idea. Louis Ellies Du Pin in 1699 says it was believed back over three centuries ago that Saul got his name from Sergius Paulus.

46. If you know the story of King Saul, the son of Kish, well, you can see all these words playing out in his life. Saul of Tarsus changed his name to Paul. Latin for *small*, Paul picks up on the question of Samuel to King Saul over a thousand years previously: 'Although you were once *small* in your own eyes, didn't you become the head of the tribes of Israel?'

Saul is a name that isn't quite as straight-forward as many commentaries suggest. Usually cited as meaning *desire*, Saul's name was prophetically spoken when he was called into his destiny by the prophet Samuel: *'To whom is all the* desire *of Israel turned, if not to you and all your father's family?'* (1 Samuel 9:20 NIV) At first Saul is diffident and apparently humble. He seems to be master of his desires. Ironically by the end of his life, desire has mastered him.

Perhaps Paul realised the dangers of an overmastering desire and obsessive zeal and this was part of his motivation for the change. Certainly he would have realised that the story of King Saul is a panorama of the Hebrew word, 'sha'uwl', *desired.* 'Sha'uwl' is the past participle of sha'al, meaning not only *desire*, but *ask*.

Sha'al also has the connotations: *borrow*, *beg*, *inquire of an oracle*, *consult a medium*, *ask of God*. Also derived from 'sha'al' is Sheol*, the underworld, the grave, the place of exile.* All the various interplays of meaning in 'sha'uwl', 'sha'al' and 'Sheol' are to be found in Saul's life.

We first hear of him *asking* after lost donkeys, we last hear of him committing suicide, not long after *consulting a medium* in an effort to draw Samuel up from *Sheol* to give an *oracle* on the upcoming battle. In between, he has the kingdom torn from him when he *asks God* for guidance and, hearing nothing, offers a sacrifice without waiting for a priest. He *begs* Samuel not to dishonour him in front of his troops. As Samuel turns to leave, Saul catches hold of the hem of his garment. As it tears, Samuel prophetically declares that, in the same way, the kingdom will be torn from Saul. Although the word used in 1 Samuel 15:27 is different, the *hem of a priest's garment* is also shuwl, sounding like Sha'uwl, Saul. No wonder Samuel saw the symbolism of the action as portentous: it tied directly to Saul's name.

47. See *Abarim Publications'* article on the *Stoics*: in Latin, the word 'pilatim' means *with pillars* and derives from the verb 'pango', meaning *to set* or *fix*, and which is also used to describe the *composing or writing or establishing of an agreement or contract*. In other words: in the mind of first century Romans, a colonnade would be construed as a visual representation of *covenant*, which is of course an idea most central to Judaism and quite befitting the Jewish temple.

It's the little details in Scripture that give us clues *something more* is going on. There are only a few places where a colonnade is mentioned: places like John 5:2 (with its five covered colonnades) and John 19:13 where Pilate (whose name is evocative of colonnade in its own right) sits in judgment over Jesus.

The Pool of Bethesda with its five colonnades seems to have been a Roman temple to the god Asclepius. And the place where Pilate sat was obviously the place where Roman justice was dispensed.

So what did a colonnade mean to the Romans? It meant 'covenant'. John was evoking that concept for a Gentile audience.

48. *Reading the Bible with Rabbi Jesus: How a Jewish Perspective Can Transform Your Understanding*, Lois Tverberg, Baker Books 2018

49. kmooreperspective.blogspot.com.au/2017/08/elymas-bar-jesus-vs-sergius-paulus.html, accessed June 2018

50. From a Christian perspective, perhaps the most intriguing example of adoption in the Roman world is

that of the British princess Gladys. She was the daughter of the tribal chieftain Caradog, who was better known by the Latin version of his name, Caractacus. For seven years Caractacus warred against Rome. After being betrayed by his mother-in-law, he was captured and eventually imprisoned in Rome. His charming daughter, Gladys, caught the eye of the emperor Claudius and was adopted by him. Renamed Claudia, she was apparently an admired beauty whose looks were praised in verse by the poet Martial. She married a senator, Rufus Pudens, and they had a son Linus. Now Claudia is not too unusual a name, nor is Linus—but Pudens is very rare. And the combination of the three names—Claudia, Linus and Pudens—is rarer still. So is this family, involving a Roman senator on the one hand and British tribal royalty on the other, mentioned in 2 Timothy 4:21? I personally think the chances they are one and the same are extremely high.

51. Zaphenanath can mean 'Anath of Zaphon', *anat of the north*, though some scholars in making Joseph a type of Jesus suggest 'Zaphenath-Paneah' means *saviour of the world*. Given the ability of Hebrew to encode more than one meaning, it is not necessary to discard either in favour of the other.

52. Also called 'Aper-'enati.

53. Wikipedia shows a picture of the seal of Aperanat. Since Scripture records a signet ring (which would actually be the device that made the seal) as being given to Joseph, I wonder if the Petrie Museum in London has an item once actually touched by Joseph, son of Jacob.

54. The name Hyksos is believed to mean *rulers of the foreign countries*. These invaders conquered most of Egypt and

ruled for about a century before being driven out. From their names and descriptions, they are believed to have been Canaanites. The Hyksos practised horse burials and horses seem to have been very important in their culture. Perhaps the mention of Joseph being given a chariot by Pharaoh alludes to this horse-loving culture.

55. See Appendix 4 for more examples. Michael Youssef in *Discover the Power of One: make your life count* points out: 'In the ancient world, a name was a person's identity. It was far more than a distinguishing label or an indicator of family heritage. A person's name said something about who the person was in character or nature. Most babies in Bible times were not named until the eighth day after their birth. This gave parents a little time to note the characteristics of their child—not only the physical ones, but the traits in their personalities and gestures that might give an indication about the nature of the child. In addition, it was a custom in Bible times that mothers spent hours singing and talking to their unborn children, bonding with them in a deep emotional and spiritual way. This bonding gave mothers special insight into the personalities and destinies of the babies in their wombs.'

Given this attitude, that name was a prophecy of identity and destiny, how strange it is for names like Jabez, *pain*, and Job, *persecution*, and Jacob, *deceiver*, and even Miriam, *bitterness*, to occur. Yet—if there were in the ancient world an expectation that this child was the one destined to overcome the unresolved family issue they had been named for—the namings seem to me to make more sense.

56. In fact, perhaps it even reveals it's hiding or covering

over additional meanings: Eprath, from 'apher' also means *covering* or *bandage* and Ephraim likewise comes from 'apher', *covering* or *bandage*.

57. Jim Stinehart at lists.ibiblio.org/pipermail/b-hebrew/2008-February/035384.html, accessed 19 April 2018

58. www.biblicaltraining.org/library/zaphenath-paneah, accessed 19 April 2018

59. www.truthunity.net/mbd/zaphenath%E2%80%93paneah, accessed 19 April 2018

60. Charles Fillmore at www.truthunity.net/mbd/zaphenath%E2%80%93paneah, accessed 19 April 2018

61. The last five translations come from creation.com/images/pdfs/tj/j27_3/j27_3_58-63.pdf, accessed 19 April 2018

62. wibab.blogspot.com.au/2007/04/28zaphenath-paneah.html, accessed 19 April 2018

63. www.studylight.org/lexicons/hebrew/6847.html, accessed 19 April 2018

64. See *God's Pottery: The Sea of Names and the Pierced Inheritance* for an explanation of the name covenant God stamped across all of creation.

65. www.eurekastreet.com.au/article.aspx?aeid=51276#.WX04ILYRVdg The irony, of course, is that the very concept of reification may itself be an example of reification.

66. In fact, Jesus could continue with the puns and jokes when some seventeen centuries later, He met Nathanael.

He said: 'Here is a true man of Israel in whom there is no Jacob.' John, writing in Greek, translated it to 'Here is a true Israelite in whom there is no guile.' (John 1:47) There are two lists of disciples given in the Gospels. On the surface, they do not appear to be wholly consistent but since we know that many of the disciples had nicknames (Simon was called Cephas or Peter, Matthew was called Levi while James and John were the Boanerges, *sons of thunder*), it is possible by systematic elimination to make them consistent by equating Nathanael with Bartholomew (*son of Ptolemy*). The *possible* problem with this is that when Jesus called the disciples, he re-defined some aspect of their names. If this re-definition is the case with Nathanael too, then it seems odd that, from beginning to end, the whole of the conversation between them alludes to the name *Jacob*.

67. Having said it's unclear, let me indulge in a little speculation. My Hebrew grammar isn't up to forming a definite conclusion but let me voice my suspicions. Genesis 32:30–31 NAS records Jacob's response to his wrestle with the angel: '*Jacob named the place Peniel* [face of God], *for he said, "I have seen God face to face, yet my life has been preserved."* Now the sun rose upon him just as he crossed over Penuel, and he was limping on his thigh.' Note the two different spellings, Peniel and Penuel—reflecting a small but significant difference in the Hebrew. Although the general comment on this is that these two forms simply represent variant spellings for the same place, I believe there is a possibility that the first, Peniel, is the name drawn '*from the adversary*' and the other, Penuel, is a place-name given to match this possible name exchange with the angel. Thus, I would suggest an alternative rendering of Genesis 32:30-31: '*Jacob named Peniel* [face of God] *from his opponent, for*

he said, "I have seen God face to face, yet my life has been preserved." Now the sun rose upon him just as he crossed over Penuel [place of the face of God], and he was limping on his thigh.'

68. Hebrew year, that is.

69. *Caesarea Philippi: Banias, the Lost City of Pan*, John Francis Wilson, I.B. Tauris, 2004

70. Because of an earthquake, the water now seeps from the bedrock below.

71. The ring of fortresses which include Masada that Herod built overlooking the Dead Sea were the direct result of his fears concerning Cleopatra's territorial ambitions.

72. Forty years *later*, it was to be the scene of horrific bloodshed. The Roman general Titus, after conquering Jerusalem, eventually brought thousands of Jewish captives here. On the pretext of celebrating the birthday of his younger brother Domitian, he had many of them thrown to wild beasts or into fire, or compelled them to fight gladiatorial-style combats against one another. About 2500 died in this orgy of violence and revenge. See: *Caesarea Philippi: Banias, the Lost City of Pan*, John Francis Wilson, I.B. Tauris, 2004

73. The original name of Dan was Laish or, in some places, Leshem. It was renamed when the tribe of Dan moved from their originally assigned territory into this area and conquered Laish. It is this renaming that seems to have added the connotation of *lion*—the meaning of Laish— into names like Daniel, along with *treasure*, the meaning of Leshem.

74. Matthew 17:1 and Mark 9:2

75. Luke 9:28

76. See *God's Pottery: The Sea of Names and the Pierced Inheritance*, Anne Hamilton, Armour Books 2016

77. The language of Judea in the first century was Greek, Latin and Aramaic (as in the sign that Pilate ordered to be placed on the cross of Jesus), reflecting the history of the land. Conquered by Alexander the Great and ruled by one of his successor generals, the common language became Greek. When the Romans invaded, they didn't displace this language but added their own. And of course the Aramaic tradition persisted. Now sometimes I suspect Jesus was playing across these three languages all at once. So while Cleopatra was a Greek name, meaning *glory of the fatherland* or *keys of the fatherland*, the 'patra' aspect of it would have had resonances for the Hebrew listener: 'peter', *firstborn*, or 'peor', *opening*. She was of course killed by an asp, which would reinforce these echoes since *asp*, *cobra*, *serpent*, *python* in Hebrew were all 'pethen', related to 'peor', *opening* and to 'miphtan', *threshold* as well as words for *seduction*, *enticement* and *lure*. All evocative of Cleopatra, the queen who seduced Mark Antony as well as Julius Caesar.

    The male version of Cleopatra was Cleopas—the name of the disciple Jesus met on the road to Emmaus. From the clues scattered through several gospels, Cleopas was probably the uncle of Jesus. His name, like Cleopatra, is evocative of both a threshold and keys. Certainly, his conversation with Jesus on that occasion would have made him the go-to person for the rest of his life whenever anyone wanted to be sure of Jesus' perspective on how any particular prophecy was fulfilled by Him.

78. So 'I am' being one of the names of God, we can see that

His first word comes from His own name. His second word intimately links 'light' to that name. Perhaps this is why 'shemen', *oil*, also considered to be the source of light, contains the word 'name'. Genesis 1:1, just two verses prior, has a mathematical structure based around multiples of 111 and repeated instances of the golden ratio. This indicates covenant is integral to God's creative output and, as I have indicated in *God's Pottery: The Sea of Names and the Pierced Inheritance*, I believe the evidence points to a name covenant.

79. The word for *serpent* here is 'nachash', which from Numbers 21 is apparently another description for a seraph.

80. Used in Exodus 4:24.

81. The refusal of Moses to undertake threshold covenant had massive repercussions two generations later. His grandson, Jonathan, was responsible for the greatest single tragedy in the history of the Hebrew people— the Fall excepted. In one stroke, involving threshold covenant violation, he destroyed the tribal brotherhood Moses had welded into a unity over forty years of desert wandering. The issues—as well as how Jesus dealt with this exact incident—are spelled out in considerable detail in *God's Priority: World-Mending and Generational Testing*, Armour Books 2017.

82. Ironically, of course, he has renamed his assistant Hosea.

83. This angel apparently returns nearly forty years later. When Joshua is on the threshold of the Promised Land, he meets the Commander of the Armies of the Lord. It is unclear whether this battle leader is an angel or is Jesus Himself: '*Joshua approached Him and asked, "Are You for us or for our enemies?" "Neither," He replied. "I have now come*

as commander of the Lord's army."' (Joshua 5 :13–14 BSB) This reply suggests something similar to Exodus 23:20–23—that the angel has only one function, war, and that if Joshua disobeys him, he will turn on the Israelites. In Judges 2:1–5 NIV, this angel actually leaves the people to fend for themselves because of their disobedience: *'The angel of the Lord went up from Gilgal to Bokim and said, "I brought you up out of Egypt and led you into the land I swore to give to your ancestors. I said, 'I will never break my covenant with you, and you shall not make a covenant with the people of this land, but you shall break down their altars.' Yet you have disobeyed me. Why have you done this? And I have also said, 'I will not drive them out before you; they will become traps for you, and their gods will become snares to you.'" When the angel of the Lord had spoken these things to all the Israelites, the people wept aloud, and they called that place Bokim. There they offered sacrifices to the Lord.'*

84. 1 Kings 22:10–28

85. But there are further subtle elements in Jesus' next words to Simon: He has prayed that Peter will be able to strengthen his *brothers*—a word that in Hebrew is curiously related to that for *reeds*. Jesus had effectively petitioned the Father for Peter to receive the strength and solidity of 'Cephas', *the cornerstone*, not be like 'Cephaph', *the reed swaying in the wind*.

86. The roots and their relatives are as follows:
    Yeru from 'yarah', *foundation*
    Yeriach, *curtain* from 'yara', *quiver*
    Yara, *to shoot, archer* from 'yarah', *throw, shoot, archery*, also *afraid*
    Yerach, *month*
    Yereach, *moon*, related to Jericho

87. When we look at all three Gospel accounts of Mary pouring oil over Jesus' head and feet, we discover the depth of Hebrew poetry hidden in the scene: mar, *crying*; mar, *drop, flowing down*; more, *myrrh*; merqach, *perfume*; merqachach, *pot of ointment*; mirzach, *banquet*; marach, *rub*; marat, *polish*; *plucked off hair*; margalah, *feet*; *at the place of the feet*; mara', *filthy*; mara', *lift up*; mara', *bitterness*; mirmac, *trampling place*; mara'ashah, *at his head*; maruwq, *purification, bodily rubbing*; mirsha'ath, *wicked woman*; mirmah, *treachery, fraud*; mera', *mischief*; merea', *confidential friend*; mare' (Aramaic), *lord.* All of these words are head rhymes for Mary. And all of them are either used in the text or alluded to indirectly.

88. You might want to object at this point that 'pinnah' is not 'cephas' and 'bochan' is not 'migdol' and, if God was really wanting a name covenant here He would have used the exactly correct terminology. This is very modern, rationalistic thinking. God is a poet. He informs us of that, specifically in relation to our life's calling, in Ephesians 2:10 NAS: *'For we are His workmanship* [Greek: *poetry*], *created in Christ Jesus for good works, which God prepared beforehand, that we should walk in them.'*

   Poets create poetry—and a significant aspect of Hebrew poetry (in fact, for many commentators almost the only aspect worth mentioning) is the 'rhyming of thoughts'. Cognates—different words with the same or very similar meaning—are an integral part of Hebrew poetry. So it should be no surprise to find that God uses cognates such as pinnah/cephas and bochan/migdol as part of His poetic workmanship when it comes to names.

89. Particularly though not exclusively in the fantasy genre.

90. And it can't be too bad a mix either, because it was a finalist in the Selah Awards 2018, run by the Blue Ridge Mountains Christian Writers Conference.

91. Jeremiah 17:9 KJV

92. A statement like that needs some justification but space constraints do not allow for a detailed explanation. Suffice it to say that the covenant numbers (multiples of 111) are everywhere a signature of Yahweh and that multiples of 17 are what sets the gospels and epistles apart from all other ancient literature. See, for example, fire-of-roses.com/wp

93. See *God's Priority: World-Mending and Generational Testing*, Anne Hamilton, Armour Books 2017

94. 1 Kings 11:9

95. See *Dealing with Ziz: Spirit of Forgetting*, Anne Hamilton, Armour Books 2018. Note also that the root of 'martureo', the Greek word for *witness*, is *remembrance*. While it can have a legal connotation, it doesn't have to. It simply means *the one who remembers*.

96. See *God's Pottery: The Sea of Names and the Pierced Inheritance*, Anne Hamilton, Armour Books 2016

97. www.abarim-publications.com/Meaning/Suph.html#. WyH1EvURVdg, accessed 14 June 2018

98. Nicolas Camille Flammarion, a noted French astronomer in the late 19th and early 20th century, referred to Venus as *The Shepherd's Star*.

99. See *God's Pottery: The Sea of Names and the Pierced Inheritance*, Anne Hamilton, Armour Books 2016

100. Let's think of another obvious example: Christmas. When knowledge and understanding gets lost, it's hard to retrieve it. I feel for those people in the early centuries of Christianity who wanted to celebrate the birth of the Saviour. Birthdays weren't a big deal until around the fourth century by which time people wanted to celebrate that of Jesus as well. But, by that time, no one had any real idea. Many different dates were proposed. Eventually, it came down to two main rivals (December 25 and January 6). Notice: they are both about the same length of time either side of the first of January. (In fact, the 25 December date was back-calculated from 1 January, as being the day when Jesus was circumcised.) Many people today believe that Jesus was born about the time of Rosh Hashanah—the Jewish New Year. One of the great symbols of Rosh Hashanah is the pomegranate—a Christmas symbol still today in Greece. Makes me wonder. It's all very easy to attribute malice to people of the past and slam them for aligning the things of Jesus with pagan festivals—when, in fact, it would appear that they used the fragments of knowledge they still had to do the best they could. If I'd been around in the fourth century and realised that all that was known about the birthday of Jesus was that it was around the New Year, I'd have been part of my culture and not realised there was a difference between the Roman and Jewish New Years. In the unlikely event that my fourth-century self knew December 25 was the feastday of Mithras, the so-called 'light of the world' and 'Sol Invictus', *the invincible sun*, I'd have thought to myself: 'Yep, that confirms it for me. Must be the birthday of Jesus. He challenged all the gods. He took back the titles that the gods of the nations stole from the one true God. He re-claimed the name 'the light of the world'—and yes, He is the embodiment of

the prophecy of Malachi: He is the invincible sun who rises with healing in His wings.' Maybe 25 December is not the birthday of Jesus. But the thinking is still valid: Jesus challenged all the gods. He took back the titles that the gods of the nations stole from the one true God. He re-claimed the title 'The Light of the World' and He is the invincible 'Sun who rises with healing in His wings.'

101. See www.abarim-publications.com/Meaning/Quirinius. html#.WyuA6fURVdg, accessed June 2018

102. What of the seventh title, 'The Way, the Truth and the Life'? The title of which I am least sure is 'the way, the truth and the life' which could refer to Python Apollo of Delphi in Greece or to the Eleusinian Mysteries of Demeter also from Greece, either of which fits very well. But this would make it the only repetition of country or ethnic locality, so I'm inclined to think there may be another answer. Perhaps it's even a reference to the Tao (or dao, *way*) of Confucianism. Nonetheless, even without being able to identify the origin of the title 'The Way, the Truth and the Life', it's clear that these seven statements add up to a stunning log of claims.

103. 'Shema Yisrael Adonai eloheinu Adonai ehad.'

104. This terminology is used by both the apostle Peter and Jude, the brother of Jesus, in their epistles when they are pointing out the consequences of abusing fallen angels. '*Yet in the same way these men, also by dreaming, defile the flesh, and reject authority, and revile angelic majesties.*' (Jude 1:8 NAS) '*Daring, self-willed, they* [proud people] *do not tremble when they revile angelic majesties, whereas angels who are greater in might and power do not bring a reviling judgment against them before the Lord.*' (2 Peter 2:10–11 NAS)

105. *Rediscovering God's Church*, Derek Prince, DPM UK, 2006

106. Matthew 16:23 NIV

107. When Peter says, 'Let's go fishing,' it's not a casual thing-of-the-moment he's suggesting. The wording indicates he's saying that he wants to return to his former way of living before he met Jesus. This is about giving up, throwing in the towel and defaulting back to an old way of life.

108. Peles, *weigh*, is to do metaphorically with *judgment*. Perhaps the *trembling of a scale pan* as it weighs is the common thread that runs from *shudder* (palats) to *weigh* (peles) to *judge* (palal) to *entreat* (palal) to *deliver* (palat).

109. See *God's Panoply: The Armour of God and the Kiss of Heaven,* Armour Books 2012; and *God's Pageantry: The Threshold Guardians and the Covenant Defender*, Armour Books 2013.

110. See *God's Priority*: *World-Mending and Generational Testing* for details. I believe that Moses consistently refused the name covenant God offered him; and that only by understanding the immensity of this offer can we understand the full extent of the treachery of Moses as he enters a lodging place on the way to Egypt. God's attack only makes sense in terms of desecration of covenant. The generational outworking of this refusal by Moses can be seen in the last few chapters of Judges.

111. See *God's Priority*: *World-Mending and Generational Testing*, Anne Hamilton, Armour Books 2017

CPSIA information can be obtained
at www.ICGtesting.com
Printed in the USA
BVHW080354040222
627985BV00004B/83